AMAZING AND EXTRAORDINARY FACTS

# LONDON
# UNDERGROUND

# LONDON
## UNDERGROUND

Stephen Halliday

RYDON
PUBLISHING

A Rydon Publishing Book
35 The Quadrant
Hassocks
West Sussex
BN6 8BP
www.rydonpublishing.co.uk
www.rydonpublishing.com

New edition published by Rydon Publishing in 2024.

First published by David & Charles in 2009.
Revised edition first published by Rydon Publishing in 2015.
Reprinted in 2016, 2018.

Copyright © Rydon Publishing 2024

A CIP catalogue record for this book is available from the British Library.

ISBN: 978-1-910821-44-2

Printed in the Czech Republic by FINIDR, s.r.o

# Contents

# Introduction

**Fraud, liquidation, suicide and transportation for life:** each of these occurred in the early history of London's Underground Railway. If any author were to write a work of fiction which incorporated such bizarre chapters in its history it would be dismissed as beyond the world of fantasy. For the London Underground is not only the world's oldest underground railway. It is also the one with the most extraordinary history. Its construction involved some of our most distinguished engineers though many of them are remembered for other reasons. John Fowler helped to design the Forth Bridge but he was a prominent contributor to the construction of the first underground railways. Isambard Kingdom Brunel built the Great Western Railway but he and his equally distinguished father, Marc Brunel, carried out pioneering work without which the deep level tubes could not have been built. Sir Joseph Bazalgette built Victorian London's sewers but also made it possible for the District Line to run along the Embankment. Two prominent literary figures were also associated with the Underground – Mark Twain and Sir John Betjeman. Sir Joseph Paxton, designer of the Crystal Palace for the Great Exhibition of 1851, put forward a proposal for a railway encased in glass to solve London's transport problems which, though ingenious, was so expensive that it was rejected in favour of the Metropolitan Line which, on 9th January 1863, became the world's first underground railway. The Times, which had condemned the Line as a 'utopian, hazardous proposition' changed its tune and declared it 'the great engineering triumph of the day'.

The London Underground has also made a major contribution to our artistic heritage. Celebrated twentieth century artists like Mabel Lucie Attwell, Rex Whistler and Graham Sutherland received their first commissions from the advertising department of the Underground. Bauhaus architecture was introduced to England through the design of stations on the Northern and Piccadilly Lines. The outstanding feature of Underground art, of course, is the tube map, now an instantly recognizable symbol of London throughout the world. Its designer, Harry Beck, who conceived it in a moment of idleness, received five guineas for his trouble!

Besides the distinguished artistic achievements there are also some bizarre entries in the record. Sir Edward Watkin's Neasden Tower was designed to surpass the Eiffel Tower and to generate huge volumes of traffic for his Metropolitan Railway. Its sad remnant was blown up soon after his death to make way for Wembley stadium. Watkin also started to build the first Channel Tunnel so that his railway system, including the Metropolitan, could dispatch its passengers to Paris. Some oddities survive, including strange structures built alongside the Northern Line on the orders of Home Secretary Herbert Morrison to house the wartime government in an emergency. They are still there, odd relics of another age.

And finally there are the crooks. Leopold Redpath was one of the last to be transported to Australia, for embezzling money intended to build the Metropolitan Line. Whitaker Wright perpetrated a number of swindles to raise money to build the Bakerloo Line and committed suicide in the Law Courts after being sentenced to seven years hard labour. Charles Tyson Yerkes, having earlier been gaoled in his native America for fraud, set about taking over the London Underground and left it on the verge of bankruptcy when he died in 1905. Without such people we wouldn't have the London Underground which, with all its faults, still makes life in London possible.

All these, and much else, are covered in the pages which follow.

# The Pioneers

For more than two centuries before the development of the Underground, ideas had been put forward for dealing with London's traffic problem. Most did not progress beyond the proposal stage. One, the forerunner of today's black cabs, was successful. The basic principles of another was incorporated into the Metropolitan Railway, the first Underground service to open, although the idea itself was never actually developed. This chapter covers some of the pioneering spirits behind these early ideas.

## THE FAILURES

### George Shillibeer's *Omnibus*

On a visit to Paris in 1828 George Shillibeer, a coachbuilder, admired the *Omnibus* service which had been introduced there by Stanislas Baudry after trials in his native Nantes. Shillibeer launched a similar service in London on 4th July 1829, using his specially designed vehicle, along the *New Road*, between Paddington Green and the Angel. He offered five services daily in each direction, charging the considerable sum of one shilling and sixpence for passengers inside the coach and one shilling for those outside. His newspaper advertisements emphasized that, 'a person of great respectability attends his Vehicle as Conductor; and every possible attention will be paid to the accommodation of ladies and children'. Such reassurances were necessary for this novel form of transport as gentry were not accustomed to sharing conveyances with strangers. Sadly, the fares were too high for most and, having deposited his passengers at the Angel, Shillibeer was still leaving them to find their way into the City. Within a year Stanislas Baudry, faced with financial ruin, drowned himself in the Seine while George Shillibeer, more prudently, fled to France to escape his creditors. He later returned to England and, after a short spell in a debtors' prison, emerged to redesign his omnibus as a funeral carriage (which it always resembled) and thereby recover his fortunes.

**DID YOU KNOW?**

In 1829 the triumph of *The Rocket* in the Rainhill trials established public transport of large numbers of people as a feature of the nineteenth century.

## Moseley's *Crystal Way*

In 1855 William Moseley, an architect, put forward a scheme to the Parliamentary Select Committee on Metropolitan Communications. He proposed to build a railway below street level between St Paul's Cathedral and Oxford Circus, with a branch to Piccadilly Circus. It would be covered by a wrought-iron grid, free of traffic, along which pedestrians could walk for one penny and watch the trains beneath them. Tolls for bridges across the Thames were at this time commonplace so the idea of charging a penny to use such a footway was not outrageous. The footway itself would be enclosed within a glass canopy (hence the *Crystal* title) with shops, flats and hotels on either side. It would have been the original Victorian shopping mall. The trains would be pneumatic railways, driven by atmospheric pressure, thus generating neither steam nor smoke. The cost was estimated at £2 million. The Committee felt that this scheme, though ingenious, was not value for money and it had the additional and fatal flaw of not connecting with any of the main-line stations.

## Paxton's Great Victorian Way

A more ambitious scheme came from Sir Joseph Paxton, the creator of the Crystal Palace. In 1855 he proposed a railway 12 miles long, linking all of London's mainline termini and crossing the Thames three times. It would be built above ground and, like Moseley's, be encased by a glass arcade with shops and houses on either side. The arcade would protect residents and shoppers from the smells of smoking chimneys and the stench of sewage flowing into the reeking Thames. It would for that reason alone have been a desirable area for pedestrians and, by linking all the main termini, would have removed a great deal of traffic from the streets. Paxton argued that for the fortunate residents the atmosphere would be 'almost equal to going to a foreign climate [and] would prevent many infirm persons being obliged to go into foreign countries in the winter'! Once again a pneumatic railway was proposed and Paxton suggested that the staggering cost of £34 million for the patriotically named Great Victorian Way should be underwritten by the Treasury. The MPs, while noting its 'many features of remarkable novelty', felt that the scheme was rather too costly .

## THE SUCCESSES

### Charles Pearson's *Arcade Railway*

After the rejection of Paxton's scheme, came Charles Pearson's *Arcade Railway*. The solicitor to the City of London and MP for Lambeth, he already had two matters to his credit. He had persuaded the City authorities to admit Jews to

EXTRAORDINARY FACT

Charles Yerkes, the man who did most to bring about the London Underground was an American entrepreneur who created the Chicago 'Loop'. He was also a fraudster, a jailbird and died in debt.

# UNDERGROUND

the Freedom of the City, giving access to positions otherwise denied to them, and he had had removed from The Monument the inscription that wrongly attributed the Great Fire of 1666 to Catholics. His railway would run from Farringdon to Kings Cross in an arcade, open to the sky but below street level and with room on either side for street traffic at ground level. The City Corporation was planning to clear slum dwellings from the area north of Ludgate Circus along what was soon to become the wide and spacious Farringdon Road. Pearson estimated that 50,000 slum dwellers could be re-housed in 'artisan cottages' to the north of Kings Cross, each with its own garden. They would be reached by the 'Parliamentary Trains' which, under the Railway Regulation Act, companies were obliged to provide, travelling at a speed of at least 12 mph and charging not more than a penny a mile. Unfortunately, the money for the scheme disappeared into the hands of an officer of the Great Northern Railway, Leopold Redpath, whose nefarious activities are described elsewhere. However, Pearson's idea was later incorporated into the

## EXTRAORDINARY FACT

In 1852 Charles Pearson called a meeting at the Bishopsgate Tavern, a popular venue for raising capital, to explain his plan for his *City Central Terminus* at Farringdon. Charles Pearson's models and maps, together with his persuasive skills, had the effect of alarming an excitable preacher called Dr Cuming who told a large gathering at Smithfield, close to the path of the proposed arcade railway, that the end of the world would be hastened by the construction of underground railways burrowing into the infernal regions and upsetting the devil.

Metropolitan Railway which began at Paddington and followed his proposed route from King's Cross to the substantial terminus that Pearson had planned at Farringdon. The line opened in January 1863, the year after Pearson's death but he had lived to see construction well advanced.

## EXTRAORDINARY FACT

In 1694 some ladies hired a hackney coach and took it to Hyde Park where they 'behaved disgracefully and deliberately insulted some very distinguished people'. As a result of this behaviour, hackneys (and their successors, taxis) were banned from Hyde Park, the ban not being lifted until two hundred and forty years later.

## Captain Bailey's *Hackney Coaches*

In the seventeenth century a Captain Bailey started a service with four 'coches hacquenées' at the Maypole Inn, now the site of the church of St Mary-le-Strand. Despite opposition from the King, the idea survived and in 1654 Cromwell authorized the 'Fellowship of Master Hackney Coachman'. Five years later the Hackney Coach Office was established to issue licences and agree fares. By 1662 there were 300 licences issued for hackneys at an annual fee of £5. Hackneys enjoyed a monopoly of wheeled public transport covering the City south of the *New Road*, (now the Marylebone Road, Euston Road and Pentonville Road) and also the borough of Southwark. In 1823 David Davies of Mount Street, Mayfair, introduced a two-seater *cabriolet*, soon shortened to 'cab'. In 2008 the Metropolitan Police assumed responsibility for the Hackneys, issuing licences and administering the dreaded *knowledge* test for would-be taxi drivers. In July of that year these responsibilities passed to Transport for London. There are now about 15,000 London black cabs with over half now being zero emission capable.

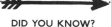

**DID YOU KNOW?**

The Hackney cab gets its name from the French *coche hacquenée*, a coach pulled by an ambling horse (a 'hack') on which the driver rode.

# The Lines

The London Underground is the oldest underground railway system in the world. The Metropolitan Railway is the oldest and the Elizabeth Line which opened in 2022 is the youngest. Each line, except the post-nationalisation Victoria, Jubilee and Elizabeth Lines, began life as a separate company, often in bitter rivalry with others. By 1933 all except the Metropolitan Railway had come under the management of the Underground Group and in that year the whole network, along with the Metropolitan and the bus companies, was absorbed by the London Passenger Transport Board. 22 million individuals use the Underground each year, making over 1.1 billion journeys. Up to 4 million journeys are made each weekday. The Central Line is the busiest, carrying about 261 million passengers each year. Kings Cross is the busiest station overall, though numbers are still well down comapred to pre-pandemic traffic.

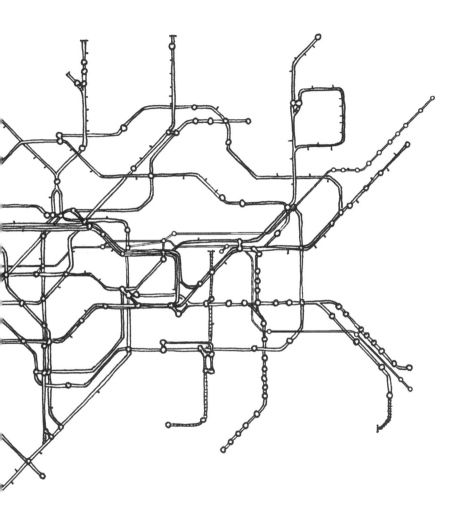

# METROPOLITAN LINE

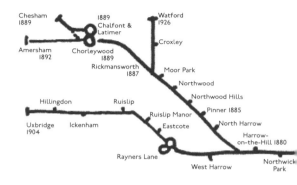

T he Metropolitan Line resulted from the combination of two separate schemes and was described by *The Times* as:

> *Utopian and one which, if it could ever be accomplished, would certainly never pay. The whole idea has been gradually associated with the plans for flying machines, warfare by balloons, tunnels under the Channel and other bold but hazardous propositions of the same kind.*

What unintended foresight that writer showed! The first element of the proposed railway was described in a Parliamentary Bill of 1854 as *The Metropolitan Railway, Paddington and the Great Western*

re

Park

bury

bury

easdon 1880

(Dollis Hill 1909)

Willesden Green

Lilburn

West
Hampstead

Finchley Road 1879

Swiss Cottage 1865

St John's Wood

Baker Street

Great
Portland
Street

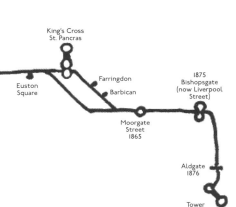

King's Cross
St. Pancras

Euston
Square

Farringdon

Barbican

1875
Bishopsgate
(now Liverpool
Street)

Moorgate
Street
1865

Aldgate
1876

Tower
Hill

### SIR JOHN FOWLER (1817–1898)

- Born in Sheffield.

- Chief engineer of the Metropolitan Railway.

- Best remembered as the designer, with Benjamin Baker, of the Forth Bridge when already famous as a civil engineer and locomotive engineer.

- An early advocate of the Metropolitan Railway, was involved in the design of both the permanent way and the locomotives.

- Later involved in promoting the Metropolitan District Railway (later the District Line), again as its consultant engineer.

- Succeeded Brunel as engineer to the Great Western Railway.

- Later involved in the design of Victoria station.

- And in building railways in Europe, India, Africa, the USA and Australia.

*Railway, the General Post Office, the London and North Western Railway and the Great Northern Railway*, the cumbersome title reflecting the aim of linking Paddington, Euston and Kings Cross. The second element was Charles Pearson's Arcade Railway from Kings Cross to Farringdon, which had been only briefly delayed by the infamous Leopold Redpath embezzling the funds.

**DID YOU KNOW?**

The oldest *structure* in use on the network was not built for the Underground and predates it by 20 years. This is the Thames Tunnel which carries the East London Line between Wapping and Rotherhithe. Built as a pedestrian tunnel by Sir Marc Brunel, it opened in 1843.

The name of the combined enterprise was mercifully shortened to Metropolitan Railway.

## Disaster strikes

The construction method adopted was 'Cut and Cover': dig a trench beneath the Marylebone Road – Euston Road – Pentonville Road – Farringdon Road, build the railway and cover it over. As work progressed the press became more favourably disposed to the new railway, even when disaster struck. When the river Fleet burst in upon the construction works along the Farringdon Road the *Illustrated London News* informed its visitors that the scene

of devastation was 'well worthy of
a visit' and when the line opened,
on 9th January 1863, *The Times*, in
contrast to its earlier warnings about
'Utopian hazardous propositions',
declared that it was 'the great
engineering triumph of the day'.

The 70-year-old Prime Minister Lord Palmerston was invited
to the opening but declined, explaining that he 'hoped to remain
above ground a little longer'. He died two years later.

## Moving on

The Metropolitan tracks had three rails in place of the usual two.
Two were for standard gauge trains (4 feet 8½ inches); the third
was to accommodate the Great Western's 7-foot gauge so that its
trains could run direct from Bristol and Reading to the City. One
hundred and fifty nine years later, this is what The Elizabeth Line
can now do.

The Metropolitan remained independent of the rest of the
network until it was absorbed, very reluctantly, into the London
Passenger Transport Board in 1933. It electrified its services from
1905, though the section beyond Amersham remained steam
operated until its transfer to British Rail in September 1961.

## SIR JOSEPH BAZALGETTE (1819–1891)

- Chief Engineer to the Metropolitan Board of Works established in 1856 as London's first Metropolitan government, replacing the network of quarrelling parishes which had governed London outside the City's square mile since mediaeval times.

- Built the system of main sewers which, by intercepting London's sewage and conducting it to treatment works at Barking and Crossness, protected London's water supply and turned the Thames from a stinking open sewer carrying waterborne epidemics like cholera and typhoid into a clean river.

- Also built the Victoria, Albert and Chelsea Embankments, thereby replacing the sewage-laden foreshores of the river with 52 acres of riverside land.

- Constructed three bridges across the river at Putney, Hammersmith and Battersea. Created numerous streets and parks including Shaftesbury Avenue, Charing Cross Road, Northumberland Avenue, Queen Victoria Street and Southwark Park.

# THE DISTRICT LINE

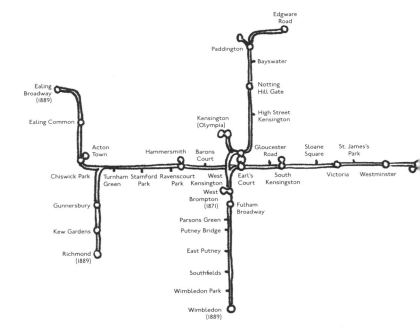

The District Line was first conceived as an offshoot of the Metropolitan Railway and was originally called the Metropolitan District Railway. The Blackfriars extension ran beneath the Victoria Embankment which had been reclaimed from the sewage-strewn foreshore of the Thames by Sir Joseph Bazalgette in the course of his construction of London's system of intercepting sewers. The real prize, however, was to create a

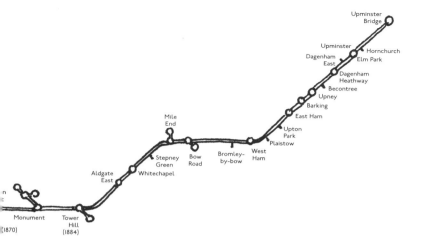

Upminster Bridge

Upminster    Hornchurch
Dagenham     Elm Park
East
Dagenham
Heathway
Becontree
Upney
Barking
East Ham
Upton
Park
Plaistow
West
Ham
Bromley-
by-bow
Bow
Road
Mile
End
Stepney
Green
Whitechapel
Aldgate
East

Monument    Tower
Hill
(1870)      (1884)

## QUICK FACTS

- The District Line opened between South Kensington and Westminster on Christmas Eve 1868.
- It was planned to join it to the Metropolitan Railway to create a 'Circle' line connecting London's mainline terminus stations north of the river.
- This happened in 1884, the two lines joining at Tower Hill.
- The extensions to Richmond, Ealing and Wimbledon ran for much of the way over the tracks of the London and South-Western Railway.
- The District Line later extended eastwards alongside the tracks of the London, Tilbury and Southend Railway to Upminster and even Southend, though the latter service was later withdrawn.
- It carries some 208 million passengers each year.
- It serves 60 stations over 40 miles of track.

'Circle' line by joining it to the Metropolitan which was eventually achieved in September 1884 but not before the two lines had become bitter rivals, a hostility that owed much to the differing personalities of their two chairmen, Sir Edward Watkin and James Staats Forbes. It was helped by a contribution of £800,000 from the City authorities and a temporary armistice between Watkin and Forbes, negotiated by an engineering contractor called Charles Lucan who persuaded the two men to meet on the neutral ground of his City office. As emollient as Watkin was aggressive, Forbes believed that 'more flies are caught by sugar than by vinegar' and placated shareholders by 'the delicacy of his touch, his light banter and personal charm', this being compared by the *Railway News* with Watkin's strategy of hectoring and bullying shareholders.

UNDERGROUND

## JAMES STAATS FORBES (1823-1904)

- Born in Aberdeen.

- Spent much of his working life rescuing railways reduced to penury by incompetent predecessors.

- Worked as a young man for Isambard Kingdom Brunel in the construction of the Great Western Railway.

- Refused the post of General Manager at the enormous salary of £10,000, probably deterred by the prospect of working with the notoriously irascible Brunel.

- Rescued a Dutch railway from insolvency and went on to do the same for the London, Chatham and Dover Railway and for the District Railway.

- Chaired District Railway from 1872 to 1901.

- Spent much of his energy protecting it from the designs of Sir Edward Watkin chairman of the Metropolitan Railway and of the South-Eastern Railway.

# THE BAKERLOO LINE

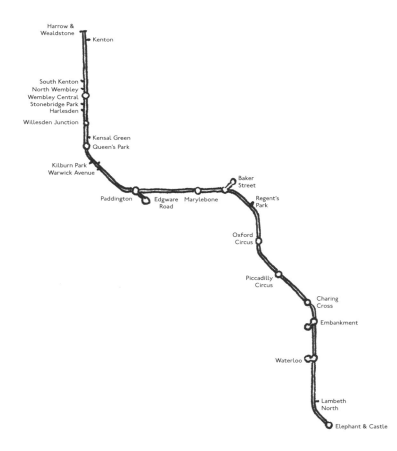

## BANKRUPTCY

Several schemes had been put forward for a link between Waterloo and Baker Street, but the finance was not forthcoming for the project until a mining engineer called Whitaker Wright (1845-1904) stepped into the breach. The line was fiercely opposed by Sir Edward Watkin who complained that 'a little electric omnibus line like this is to block big companies with millions and millions of money' because he feared that it would interfere with his grand ambition to build a railway from Manchester to Paris. His protests were in vain. In 1897 Wright approached the directors of the fledgling line and offered to raise the finance they needed to begin work, an offer they accepted with relief. Wright opened an office in the City, trading as the *London and Globe Finance Corporation* which raised £700,000 for the new line. Construction work began in August 1898 and proceeded for 18 months at a cost of £650,000. Meanwhile, Wright attempted to 'rig' the market by buying up Globe shares which resulted in losses, then trying to unload shares in the still embryonic railway on to the market. This strategy

**DID YOU KNOW?**
About 55 per cent of the Underground is in fact *overground*.

failed, as did a wildly optimistic speech to shareholders as the company sank further into chaos. On 28th December 1900 the London and Globe was declared bankrupt and construction ceased. Wright fled to France. A determined creditor, however, succeeded in obtaining an arrest warrant from a judge and Wright, having by now fled to New York, was arrested and charged with fraud.

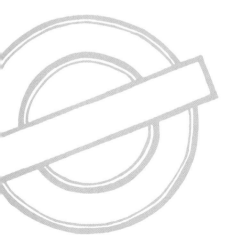

**EXTRAORDINARY FACT**
In July 2008 a Cambridge student travelled the length of the network to raise £800 for cancer research. He boarded a train at 4.59 am on Monday, 29th July, at Upminster and ended his journey at Amersham at 1.52 am the following day, 20 hours and 53 minutes later.

# PENAL SERVITUDE AND SUICIDE

On 26th January 1904 Wright was convicted of defrauding investors of £5 million through the use of fraudulent accounts and balance sheets and, in the words of Mr Justice Bingham, sentenced to, 'The severest punishment which the Act permits, that you go to penal servitude for seven years'. Wright left the courtroom proclaiming his innocence and his intention to appeal. He handed his watch to his solicitor explaining, 'I will not need this where I am going' and moments later he collapsed, dead from a cyanide capsule he had been carrying. He was buried in the grounds of his palatial mansion at Lea Park, Witley, Surrey amid his landscaped gardens, private theatre, observatory, lakes and an underwater billiard hall encased in thick glass, still existing in a somewhat decrepit state. His entry in the *Dictionary of National Biography* comments:

> *His abilities as a public speaker were turned to good account at shareholders' meetings and inspired confidence in his most disastrous undertakings.*

One is reminded of the activities of the late Robert Maxwell. Upon such men as Whitaker Wright was the London Underground dependent in the early days of the twentieth century and his legacy was soon to be taken over by the even more flamboyant figure of Charles Tyson Yerkes.

> **AMAZING FACT**
>
> Whitaker Wright was able to carry into the courtroom, concealed on his person, a loaded revolver and a cyanide capsule, which he used to kill himself immediately after being sentenced to seven years penal servitude on 26th January 1904.

# THE CIRCLE LINE

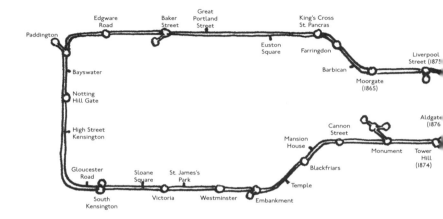

## QUICK FACTS

- The Circle Line was created in 1884 by the junction of the Metropolitan Railway and the District Railway, later the District Line, at Tower Hill.
- The line did not run smoothly in its early days and hostility between the two companies was renewed.
- It carries some 115 million passengers each year.
- The Circle Line serves 27 stations over 14 miles of track.

On 28 March 1905 the first successful trial run of an electric train took place from Mill Hill Park (Acton Town) along the southern section of the Inner Circle. The electrification of the line was completed on 1st July, 1905.

The highly desirable development of creating the Circle Line by joining the Metropolitan and District Lines had been long delayed by the financial problems of the District Railway and the mutual hostility of the two chairmen. The chairman of the District was James Staats Forbes, who specialised in rescuing unprofitable railways, of which the District was a fine example. It was barely profitable and rarely paid a dividend to its long-suffering shareholders. The chairman of the Metropolitan Railway was the more flamboyant Sir Edward Watkin who, when not planning a railway from Manchester to Paris, devoted his time to insulting his own shareholders and deriding his rivals, especially James Staats Forbes.

**DID YOU KNOW?**

It takes, on average, one hour to travel the whole of the Circle Line.

The completion of the long-promised Circle was not greeted with enthusiasm in every quarter. *The Railway Times*, which had long questioned the value of the project, printed a leading article headed 'The Inner Circle Delusion' a week after it opened describing it as an example of 'aerial castles, pleasing to the imaginative mind'. It also reported Circle trains ran hours late and that one group of passengers staged a breakout from a solitary train marooned between stations: 'the deluded passengers who have paid their fare make a financial sacrifice and stampede over the banks in search of some more reliable conveyance'.

**EXTRAORDINARY FACT**

At the official opening of the Circle Line the chairmen of the two companies, who loathed each other, were obliged to share a carriage. They managed to do this without exchanging a single word.

### SIR EDWARD WATKIN (1819–1901)

- Born in Northenden, Lancashire.

- As the chairman of four railway companies he was known as 'the second railway king' after George Hudson, the famous Yorkshire railway promoter, whose career was ruined by a financial scandal.

- Soon acquired a reputation for his involvement in the development of rail networks in four continents.

- Made a contribution to the building of the great Canadian Pacific Railway 1885, one of the finest engineering triumphs of the 19th century.

- Helped with the first serious attempt to create the Channel Tunnel, founding the Channel Tunnel Company, which was authorised by an Act of Parliament in 1875.

- Following a visit to Paris in 1889, attempted to build a structure bigger than the 894-foot Eiffel Tower. Watkin's tower was abandoned after reaching 155 feet. The site eventually became Wembley Stadium, and was originally given the nickname Watkin's Folly.

An argument about how many trains each company should be allowed to run round the Circle was not resolved by an agreement for one to run clockwise and the other anti-clockwise, since each then accused the other of sending passengers 'the wrong (i.e. the long) way' round the system. An early, comical incident, involved a dispute over which company had the right to occupy a siding at South Kensington station, where the District left its locomotives. The Metropolitan removed them. The District chained its engines to the rails. The

Metropolitan sent one, two and finally three locomotives to haul them away. In August 1884 the West London Advertiser announced that 'A tug-of-war ensued in which the chained train came off the victor'.

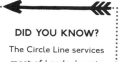

# THE CENTRAL LINE

>>>>

**DID YOU KNOW?**

Mark Twain attended the opening of the
Central line on 27th June 1900.

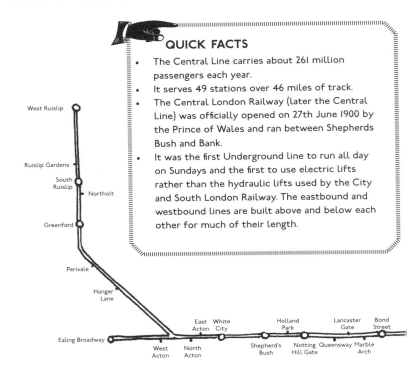

**QUICK FACTS**

- The Central Line carries about 261 million passengers each year.
- It serves 49 stations over 46 miles of track.
- The Central London Railway (later the Central Line) was officially opened on 27th June 1900 by the Prince of Wales and ran between Shepherds Bush and Bank.
- It was the first Underground line to run all day on Sundays and the first to use electric lifts rather than the hydraulic lifts used by the City and South London Railway. The eastbound and westbound lines are built above and below each other for much of their length.

West Ruislip

Ruislip Gardens

South Ruislip

Northolt

Greenford

Perivale

Hanger Lane

Ealing Broadway

West Acton

North Acton

East Acton

White City

Shepherd's Bush

Holland Park

Notting Hill Gate

Queensway

Lancaster Gate

Marble Arch

Bond Street

The *Daily Mail* report of the opening of the Central Line wrote of 'voracious curiosity, astonished satisfaction and solid merit. If this kind of thing goes on London will come to be quite a nice place to travel in…the conductor was all of a quiver of joy and pride. But there was no indecorous exhibition of emotion. Every man was solidly British'.

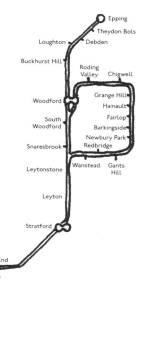

Epping
Theydon Bols
Loughton
Debden
Buckhurst Hill
Roding Valley
Chigwell
Woodford
Grange Hill
Hainault
South Woodford
Fairlop
Barkingside
Newbury Park
Redbridge
Snaresbrook
Wanstead
Gants Hill
Leytonstone
Leyton
Stratford
Bethnal Green
Mile End
Liverpool Street
Chancery Lane
St. Paul's
Bank
Monument

**DID YOU KNOW?**

The platforms at Redbridge station, on the Central Line, are closest to the surface, being only 26 feet below the road.

The opening of the Central Line prompted an effusion of enthusiasm from the press. The normally staid *Railway Times* reported that the new line had had such a calming effect on London's traffic that the number of road accidents and traffic offences had plunged. Unlike the other lines it did not stop for a 'church interval' on Sundays. The tracks through its platforms were laid in a shallow 'hump' to help trains slow down as they entered the station and accelerate as they left, a feature which is still evident to the observant waiting passenger and particularly noticeable at St Paul's station. Another distinguishing feature of the Central is that the tracks run above each other rather than side by side. This was designed to ensure that the line followed the street above and did not pass beneath buildings, thereby avoiding the danger

**EXTRAORDINARY FACT**

Because of the flat rate fare of two pence the Central Line became known as '*The Tuppeny Tube*'. *The Railway Times* reported that a young woman suffering from anorexia, 'suddenly developed a ravenous appetite after a single journey by the new underground railway vulgarly known as the *Twopenny Tube*'.

UNDERGROUND

The Central Line employed much more powerful locomotives than the original 'tube' and the weight of the locomotives and rolling stock caused such vibrations above that draughtsmen in offices in Cheapside complained that they were unable to draw straight lines on their drawing-boards. The Board of Trade duly set up a 'Vibration Committee' headed by Sir John Wolfe-Barry, designer of Tower Bridge, who recommended better suspension for the locomotives.

of litigation concerning damage to foundations. The line featured in a 1900 revival of Gilbert and Sullivan's *Patience* with a reference to a 'Tuppeny Tube young man'. In 1908 it was extended to White City where it served visitors to the Franco-British exhibition of that year and to the first London Olympics which were held there over a period of six months.

Ealing was reached, via Great Western tracks, in the 1920s but the major expansion of the line occurred in the 1930s and 1940s when it reached Ruislip and Epping.

# THE NORTHERN LINE

The Northern Line was built to link the City and South London Railway and the Charing Cross, Euston and Hampstead Railway at Euston. The City and South London was opened on 4th November 1890 by the Prince of Wales, running from King William Street station (now closed) just north of London Bridge to Stockwell, three and a half miles to the south. The distinctive dome-like structure that surmounts Northern Line stations like Stockwell was constructed to accommodate the mechanism of the lifts, an innovation at the time.

## QUICK FACTS

- The Northern Line was created in 1924.
- It was the first line to use lifts to reach the platforms.
- It was the first deep-level tube built with the use of a tunnelling shield.
- The Northern Line carries about 252 million passengers each year.
- It serves 50 stations over 36 miles of track.

### DID YOU KNOW?

The highest point on the network is the Dollis Brook Viaduct over Dollis Road on the Mill Hill East branch of the Northern Line where the tracks are 60 feet above the ground.

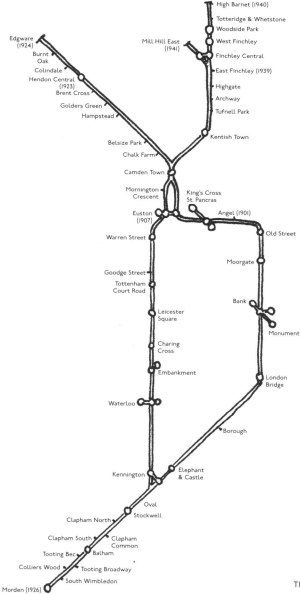

High Barnet (1940)
Totteridge & Whetstone
Woodside Park
West Finchley
Mill Hill East (1941)
Finchley Central
East Finchley (1939)
Highgate
Archway
Tufnell Park
Edgware (1924)
Burnt Oak
Colindale
Hendon Central (1923)
Brent Cross
Golders Green
Hampstead
Belsize Park
Chalk Farm
Kentish Town
Camden Town
Mornington Crescent
King's Cross St. Pancras
Angel (1901)
Euston (1907)
Warren Street
Old Street
Moorgate
Goodge Street
Tottenham Court Road
Bank
Leicester Square
Monument
Charing Cross
Embankment
London Bridge
Waterloo
Borough
Kennington
Elephant & Castle
Oval
Stockwell
Clapham North
Clapham South
Clapham Common
Tooting Bec
Balham
Colliers Wood
Tooting Broadway
South Wimbledon
Morden (1926)

**DID YOU KNOW?**

Waterloo has the largest number of escalators, 23, together with 2 moving pavements ("travelators"). It needs them to move the vast number of passengers that arrive in the morning peak period 7.00 to 10.00.

As distinct from the earlier 'cut and cover' lines like the Metropolitan and District, the Northern Line is a deep-level tube and the first to be built with the aid of a tunnelling shield. It used electric locomotives from the start and had narrower tunnels than other lines which had to be widened when it was linked to the other component of the Northern Line, the Charing Cross, Euston and Hampstead Railway. The latter was the creation of Charles Tyson Yerkes and opened on 22nd June 1907 running from Charing Cross via Euston and Camden Town to Highgate (later renamed Archway) and Golders Green. The first train through the link between the two components of the Northern Line was driven (under supervision) by a sixteen-year old boy called Anthony Bull whose father was MP for Hampstead. He presumably enjoyed the experience since he later joined London Transport and became its vice-chairman before giving this account to the present author at the age of 92.

**AMAZING FACT**

Northern Line's Hampstead station has the deepest lift shaft at 181 feet and the system's deepest point below ground is a short distance to the north, below Hampstead Heath, where the Northern Line is 221 feet below ground.

## CHARLES TYSON YERKES (1837–1905)

- Born in Philadelphia in 1837.

- Began his business career as a clerk in a grain commission house, before becoming a broker when he was 21 years old. He lost his fortune following the Great Chicago fire of 1871 and was imprisoned for some months, reputedly for embezzlement.

- Persuaded by R. W. Perks, the ex-solicitor for the Metropolitan Railway, to finance the electrification of the District Railway in London.

- By March 1901, Yerkes had control of the District Line. Forming the Metropolitan District Electric Traction Company (M.D.E.T) in July of that year, raised £1 million of capital in America to invest in the company.

- The M.D.E.T. acquired control of the Brompton and Piccadilly Tube as well as the C.C.E&H.R. in September 1901.

# THE EAST LONDON LINE

The intention behind the building of the East London Line was to provide a link between main-line railways north and south of the river. However, poor connections, especially to the north, meant that the link was never fully effective. Within ten years of opening, the line experienced serious financial difficulties as

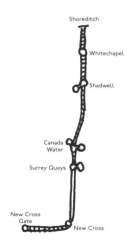

a result of placing its fortunes in the hands of a colourful financier called Albert Grant.

Grant made early use of the Penny Post for the technique of direct mailing by which he induced small investors such as clergymen and widows to invest in enterprises which promised fabulous returns. These included The Cadiz Waterworks, the Labuan Coal Company and the Emma Silver Mine (the location of the last two remaining for ever a mystery). Grant raised £1 million for the Emma Silver Mine but the £20 shares quickly declined to a value of one shilling (5p) when the promised silver (and indeed the mine) failed to appear. Grant himself made £100,000 commission on the deal. He insisted on being addressed as 'Baron Grant' after being made an hereditary baron of the Kingdom of Italy for helping to raise money for a shopping centre in Milan.

The East London Railway was one of many organisations (and people) which regretted their attempts to raise funds through Grant. In the words of a later writer, 'Nearly all of the flotations in which Grant had a hand in the 1860s led to legal disputes involving allegations of fraud.' It was just such a fraud that undermined the East London Railway's attempts to raise capital. This misfortune led to the appointment as chairman of Sir Edward Watkin who restored its finances and attempted to incorporate it in a network of railways, all chaired by him, to provide a full route from Manchester to Dover and thence, via his proposed Channel Tunnel, on to Paris. The main claim to fame of this small corner of the underground network is that it runs through Marc Brunel's Thames Tunnel, opened in 1843 as a foot tunnel between Wapping and Rotherhithe and the first tunnel ever to be built beneath a river. The Brunel Engine House Museum, adjacent to Rotherhithe station to the south of the Thames, tells the story of the creation of the tunnel.

**DID YOU KNOW**

A channel tunnel wa█ planned as early as 18█ by the Chairman of t█ East London Railway█ Sir Edward Watkin.

**ALBERT GRANT (1830-1899)**

- Born Abraham Gottheimer in Dublin, the son of a pedlar.

- Changed his name to Grant in 1863 and embarked upon a very successful career (for himself) as a company promoter.

- Elected MP for Kidderminster in 1865 but was unseated following allegations of bribery.

- Spent £28,000 buying and refurbishing the derelict Leicester Square whose central feature is a statue of Shakespeare which bears an inscription recording the gift of the square to the people of London by Albert Grant.

- Died in penury in 1899 after one last extravagance – a 'Bachelors Ball' at a huge house he built in Kensington which was promptly seized by creditors who sold the house's ornate staircase to Madame Tussaud's, where it remains.

# THE PICCADILLY LINE

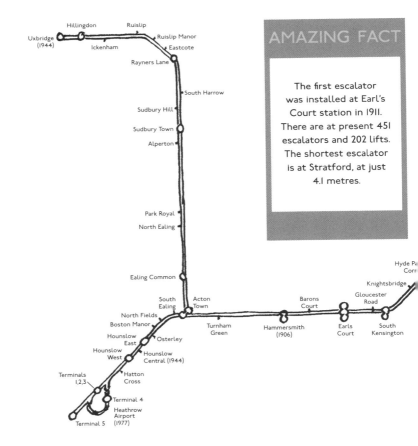

Hillingdon
Ruislip
Uxbridge (1944)
Ruislip Manor
Ickenham
Eastcote
Rayners Lane
South Harrow
Sudbury Hill
Sudbury Town
Alperton
Park Royal
North Ealing
Ealing Common
South Ealing
Acton Town
North Fields
Boston Manor
Turnham Green
Hammersmith (1906)
Barons Court
Earls Court
Gloucester Road
Knightsbridge
South Kensington
Hyde Park Corner
Hounslow East
Osterley
Hounslow West
Hounslow Central (1944)
Hatton Cross
Terminals 1,2,3
Terminal 4
Heathrow Airport
Terminal 5 (1977)

## AMAZING FACT

The first escalator was installed at Earl's Court station in 1911. There are at present 451 escalators and 202 lifts. The shortest escalator is at Stratford, at just 4.1 metres.

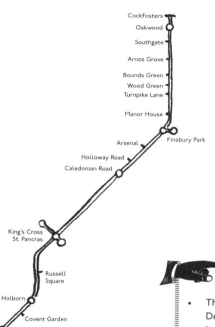

Cockfosters
Oakwood
Southgate
Arnos Grove
Bounds Green
Wood Green
Turnpike Lane
Manor House
Finsbury Park
Arsenal
Holloway Road
Caledonian Road
King's Cross St. Pancras
Russell Square
Holborn
Covent Garden
Leicester Square

## QUICK FACTS

- The Piccadilly Line opened on 15th December 1906.
- It ran from Hammersmith to Finsbury Park and was largely financed by American investors.
- In 1907 a branch-line was opened from Holborn to Strand (later renamed Aldwych) but the station was little used and closed in 1994.
- The Piccadilly Line carries about 210 million passengers each year.
- It serves 52 stations over 44 miles of track.

Originally The Great Northern, Piccadilly and Brompton Railway, the Piccadilly Line opened following some devious financial manoeuvring by its promoter, Charles Tyson Yerkes, who had outwitted his fellow-American J.P.Morgan, advocate of a rival scheme. In the 1930s serious problems of overcrowding arose at Finsbury Park where passengers changed from underground services to buses and trams amid chaotic scenes. The Vice-chairman of the Underground Group, Frank Pick, argued that the line should be extended to Cockfosters to relieve this congestion but the London and North-Eastern Railway (LNER) objected on the grounds that it would lose much of its suburban traffic. The LNER was over-ruled and Cockfosters was reached in 1933, many of its new stations later achieving the status of listed buildings as outstanding examples of Underground Architecture.

**DID YOU KNOW?**

Angel station on the Northern Line has the longest escalators in the UK, taking 80 seconds to carry their passengers their length of 197 feet.

## LONGEST AND SHORTEST

- The London Underground is the third most extensive network in the world, with 251 miles of track serving 272 stations.

- The Elizabeth Line is the longest, with 73 miles of track serving 41 stations.

- The longest journey that can be made without changing trains is from West Ruislip to Epping on the Central Line, a distance of just over 34 miles.

- The longest tunnel is between East Finchley and Morden, via Bank, at 17.25 miles.

- The shortest distance between adjacent stations is between Leicester Square and Covent Garden on the Piccadilly Line, about 260 metres.

- The longest distance between stations is the 3.9 miles from Chalfont & Latimer to Chesham on the Metropolitan Line.

# THE VICTORIA LINE

## QUICK FACTS

- The Victoria Line opened to passengers in 1968.
- It was the first new tube line to be built for 60 years.
- The Victoria Line was the first to adopt a form of Automatic Train Operation whereby the driver starts the train and operates the doors while the speed and braking are operated by trackside signals.
- It carries some 200 million passengers each year.
- The Victoria Line serves 16 stations over 13 miles of track.

The Victoria Line was first proposed in a London transportation plan of 1943 and by 1952 it had become known as 'Route C' but, despite the acute congestion associated with heavier car use in London, it had to wait for ten years before obtaining authorisation from the Treasury. The name 'Victoria Line' was the suggestion of David McKenna, London Transport's Chief Commercial Officer. Ingenious governmental prevarication followed, one minister asking whether the investment 'would pay a better dividend were it spent on off-street parking'! The line was rescued by two developments. The first was a new way of appraising investment projects by 'cost-benefit analysis', pioneered by two academics from Oxford University and the London School of Economics. This took account of the benefits in time saved that would accrue to other travellers, such as motorists and bus passengers, from the reduced congestion that the new line would offer. The other development was unemployment. In 1962 Harold Macmillan's government was worried by the growing number of jobless, especially in the north of England. Sir John Elliot, the energetic chairman of London Transport, advised the government that tunnel segments for the new line could be ordered from North-East shipyards and would also create many jobs in construction in the London area.

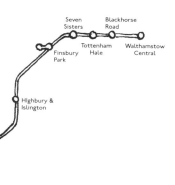

Seven Sisters
Blackhorse Road
Tottenham Hale
Walthamstow Central
Finsbury Park
Highbury & Islington
King's Cross St Pancras
Euston
Warren Street
Oxford Circus
Green Park
Victoria
Pimlico
Vauxhall
Stockwell
Brixton (1971)

AMAZING FACT

Because it would link two of London's busiest stations, Kings Cross and Victoria, the inelegant name 'KingVic' was at one time considered for the new line.

# THE JUBILEE LINE

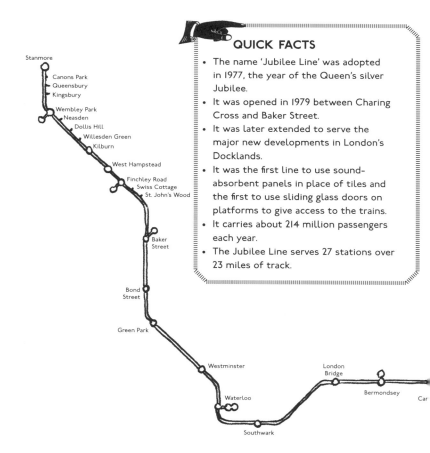

## QUICK FACTS

- The name 'Jubilee Line' was adopted in 1977, the year of the Queen's silver Jubilee.
- It was opened in 1979 between Charing Cross and Baker Street.
- It was later extended to serve the major new developments in London's Docklands.
- It was the first line to use sound-absorbent panels in place of tiles and the first to use sliding glass doors on platforms to give access to the trains.
- It carries about 214 million passengers each year.
- The Jubilee Line serves 27 stations over 23 miles of track.

Stanmore
Canons Park
Queensbury
Kingsbury
Wembley Park
Neasden
Dollis Hill
Willesden Green
Kilburn
West Hampstead
Finchley Road
Swiss Cottage
St. John's Wood
Baker Street
Bond Street
Green Park
Westminster
Waterloo
Southwark
London Bridge
Bermondsey
Car

The Jubilee Line, like the Victoria Line, was originally proposed in the 1950s but had to wait even longer to be born. It was authorized in 1972 as 'The Fleet Line' but, as construction gathered pace, the new name was chosen. The original concept of the line was to provide an alternative access to the City but this was abandoned in favour of a route south of the river, an area poorly served by the Underground while absorbing the Baker Street – Stanmore section from the Bakerloo Line. The Docklands extension was awarded the title *Millennium Building of the Year* by the Royal Fine Art Commission Trust and many of the stations on the extension are models of modern design. The innovative use of sliding doors and sound-absorbent panels on platforms make the Jubilee Line much quieter than other Underground lines.

**DID YOU KNOW?**

Until the East London line ceased being part of the underground, The Jubilee Line was the only line to connect with all the others on the network (now the Central line does too).

Stratford

West Ham

Canning Town

North Greenwich

Wharf

## AMAZING FACT

Westminster station, which opened as part of the Jubilee Line extension in 1999, was, at the time, the country's most complicated excavation. Many of the new stations on the line have received architectural awards.

# THE ELIZABETH LINE

O n 23rd February 2016 Her Majesty Queen Elizabeth II unveiled a plaque at Bond Street station revealing that London's new underground railway, Crossrail, would be named The Elizabeth Line in her honour and that the colour of the new line on underground maps would be, appropriately, the royal purple.

As the Queen unveiled the plaque it was predicted that the new line would enter service in the autumn of 2019 at a cost of £15 billion. Alas this was far from the truth. Problems with signalling and the completion of the huge stations required by the trains, meant that the final bill was nearer £19 billion and it finally opened on 24th May 2022.

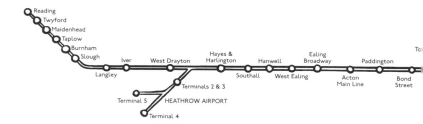

It is nevertheless an extraordinary feat of engineering and means that passengers can now travel from Reading and Heathrow in the West to Shenfield in Essex and Abbey Wood in Kent, passing through 26 miles of new tunnels beneath London. With the line now reaching new platforms at Paddington it echo's its Victorian predecessors whose trains from Brunel's GWR joined the Metropolitan line in January 1863; while at Tottenham Court Road the new tunnels will be threaded beneath escalators 12 inches above and the Northern Line platforms 36 inches beneath it. Farringdon, the original terminus of the Metropolitan Railway, will again be a major hub of the system, connecting with Thameslink as well as the Metropolitan and Circle Lines. The line is a magnificent addition to the world's oldest Underground Railway.

## BOND STREET

Bond Street is a name found on the Underground map and the Monopoly board but not on the *A to Z*. The Southern section, from Piccadilly, is called Old Bond Street and the Northern link to Oxford Street is named New Bond Street. But what's in a name for a road that passes through the heart of Mayfair, Monopoly's most expensive destination?

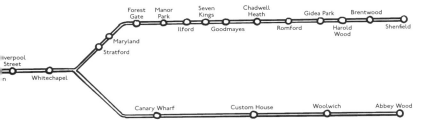

# Financing the Underground

Financing underground railways has always been difficult and from the early days the problem attracted the attention of optimistic, incompetent and sometimes dishonest financiers (several of them, paradoxically, from impeccable Quaker and Methodist backgrounds). Building railways, especially below ground, is costly and the interest on the capital expenditure has always been a millstone round the necks of managers and shareholders. Without the sometimes unconventional activities of financiers like Charles Yerkes, Sir Edgar Speyer and Whitaker Wright the early network would never have been built.

## CHARLES YERKES

### Death of 'The Titan' in New York

On 29th December 1905 the railway entrepreneur and financier Charles Tyson Yerkes (rhymes with 'turkeys') died in New York, having become involved in 1900 in the development of the London Underground  He did not die in his magnificent Fifth Avenue mansion but in the almost equally opulent surroundings of the Waldorf-Astoria hotel. His mansion, together with the gold bedstead he had purchased from the King of Belgium, was at that time occupied by his estranged wife. The mansion, the bed and his collection of Old Masters were bequeathed to the citizens of New York but this legacy proved to be of no value to the intended beneficiaries since Yerkes' many creditors claimed the monies he owed them.

## Yerkes in America

Born in Philadelphia in 1837 to a Quaker family, he quickly rose to a prominent position in that city. His ability to persuade his fellow citizens to buy municipal bonds was not matched by his ability to manage his financial commitments, a weakness which led to an early prison sentence for embezzlement. Upon release he proceeded to Chicago, applying his talents to the financing and construction of the transport system, including the famous 'Loop' railway. He was inventive in his methods of dealing with competitors. He would buy stock cheaply when a company was first floated and then, when the new company was negotiating loans, Yerkes would unload his stock suddenly on the stock exchanges, causing the price to fall. At the same time he would plant stories in the press about the company's financial stability, reaping a profit on the sale of his own shares while making it difficult or impossible for the competitor to raise the additional capital required.

## Bribery

He maintained his monopoly on Chicago transportation and ensured toleration of poor conditions for the travelling public by bribing the City Fathers. Eventually a new City Council resolved to dismantle Yerkes' empire which had earned the name 'The Chicago Traction Tangle'.

**AMAZING FACT**

Yerkes' notoriety was such that he features, barely disguised, in a series of novels by the American writer Theodore Dreiser, including *The Titan* which features a power-hungry business tycoon.

## The Methodist and the Quaker

In the end, much of the London Underground
was born out of a partnership between
this licentious lapsed Quaker and a devout
Methodist. Yerkes' plan to take London's
transport system in hand as he had Chicago's
originated in his improbable friendship with
Robert Perks, a Methodist. He formed a
partnership with the pious Perks which was
to have a decisive influence on London's
Underground Railway system. Perks had a substantial shareholding
in London's ailing District Railway (now the District Line) He met
Yerkes during a trip to New York and, convinced that converting
the line from steam to electric traction would both reduce costs and
increase the number of passengers, asked the American to bring his
financial acumen to bear upon the fortunes of the District.

## Yerkes in London: rumour and rascality

Yerkes arrived in London in 1901 having raised the best part of
£1 million. As the work progressed, Yerkes' ambitions extended to
other railway projects and he founded the Underground Electric
Railways of London Ltd. He now began to further an even
more ambitious project to gain control over most of London's
underground railway network. By March 1902 Yerkes owned one
ailing line (the District), one half-built one (the Bakerloo) and
two which were still on the drawing board (the Piccadilly and the
Charing Cross, Euston and Hampstead Railways).

## Electrification

In 1900 the Metropolitan Railway and the District prepared for electrification. Engineers who examined the proposals recommend a system which offered a 3,000 volt alternating current system fed to the trains through overhead wires. Yerkes did not like the system, believing it to be unproven and possibly unsafe. He advocated a system using direct current fed through conductor rails. The old hostility between the District and the Metropolitan now resurfaced, with the Metropolitan clinging to the overhead system and denouncing Yerkes in shareholders' meetings.

The dispute occupied the summer of 1901. In September the Board of Trade ruled in favour of Yerkes and the Metropolitan board, still sulking, turned down Yerkes' offer to supply them with electricity. Instead they built their own power station at Neasden while Yerkes built his station at Lots Road, Chelsea. This riverside site offered ready access to barges which would bring in the huge quantities of coal the eight generators required. The electrification of the Circle

### EMBEZZLEMENT

The Metropolitan Railway would have opened several years earlier if it were not for the activities of Leopold Redpath, an officer of the Great Northern Railway based at King's Cross. The Great Northern had set aside £170,000, originally to invest in Charles Pearson's 'Arcade Railway' to run from Paddington via King's Cross to Farringdon. When the money was required, however, it was discovered that it had been stolen by Redpath who, in the words of a contemporary account, had used it for, 'the furnishings of magnificent houses'. Redpath was one of the last convicts to be transported to Australia where, according to one of his descendants, he was a popular figure who made a new life there for himself.

Line in conjunction with the Metropolitan was completed by July 1905. Eventually Yerkes' power station supplied the whole Underground network.

## Bankruptcy threatens

Construction of the Bakerloo, Piccadilly and Hampstead Lines proceeded apace in 1902 but the company began to run out of money. Yerkes failed to raise the further £2 million that was needed. He resorted to an ingenious scheme of selling 'profit sharing notes' at a discounted price and promising a high rate of interest on redemption of the notes in three years time. The revenue forecasts upon which Yerkes had based his scheme proved to be disastrously optimistic. By June 1907 all three new lines, the Bakerloo, the Piccadilly and the Charing Cross, Euston & Hampstead were in operation but passenger numbers and hence revenues were less than half those anticipated. It was twenty years before they reached the levels on which Yerkes had based his calculations. In the meantime June 30th 1907, the date for the redemption of the 'profit-sharing notes' was approaching with no real prospect of paying the increasingly worried holders of the 'profit sharing notes'. Yerkes had died by this time, and Edgar Speyer became increasingly alarmed as his bank had invested almost £400,000. So Speyer approached George Gibb, the highly respected manager of the North-Eastern Railway to take over the management of the company.

**GEORGE GIBB** (1850-1925)

- Was General Manager of North-Eastern Railway when, in December 1905, he was approached by Edgar Speyer to manage the stricken Underground Electric Railways of London.

- Introduced statistical analysis of traffic patterns at North-Eastern Railway, which had increased the company's profitability.

- Also had experience of introducing electric traction to suburban services around Newcastle.

- Six days before Yerkes died, accepted Speyer's offer to become Managing Director of U.E.R.L at the very generous salary of £8,000 a year.

- Soon learned that the District Railway alone was losing money at the rate of £60,000 a year.

- Slashed overheads by merging the management of the four lines and brought with him **FRANK PICK** who was to have a decisive influence on the development of the network.

## Liquidation

Negotiations between Speyer and the predominantly American shareholders reached a critical point in April 1907 by which time Speyer's bank had already paid £475,000 to creditors to stave off the threat of liquidation. The American shareholders continued to cling to the idea that profitability was just around the corner but finally, a month before the June deadline, they caved in. For each £100 of profit-sharing notes they accepted £40 worth of fixed-interest bonds redeemable on 1st January 1933; and £70 of income bonds, which might or might not receive interest payments (they rarely did) and would fall due on 1st January 1948. The scheme was accepted by 96% of shareholders.

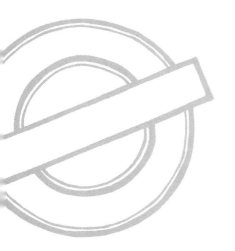

**EDGAR SPEYER (1862-1932)**

- Born in New York of German ancestry.

- Came to London in the 1880s and established himself as a banker, philanthropist and patron of the arts.

- Made substantial contributions to the running of hospitals and the early Promenade Concerts in Queen's Hall.

- Rescued London's Underground Railways from the financial machinations of Charles Tyson Yerkes.

- Took British citizenship in 1892 and was created a baronet in 1906.

- In 1914 he was accused of being a German sympathizer and of signalling to German U-boats from his home near Cromer in Norfolk.

- Offered to resign his baronetcy and his Privy Councillorship but the offer was declined by the Prime Minister on behalf of King George V.

- Nevertheless went into exile in America and died in Germany in 1932.

# UNEMPLOYMENT

In the twentieth century the network continued to struggle to gain the investment needed to maintain track, signalling, stations and rolling stock. Both as a private company and as a nationalised undertaking, it has often had to depend upon political events to attract investment and its greatest aid has come from fears of unemployment.

## A missed opportunity

The management of the network has shown great enterprise in securing funds from government in difficult circumstances. However, this is no way to run a railway and could probably have been avoided if MPs had adopted a suggestion made by Frank Pick in the 1930s. He pointed out to a Parliamentary committee that it had been necessary for the Underground to buy substantial quantities of agricultural land when extending the network into the suburbs. Pick suggested that the railways should be allowed to purchase additional land and develop it for housing, thereby recouping much of the capital expenditure. The MPs disagreed. Property development profits were for property developers, not underground railways.

## HOW THE NORTHERN, PICCADILLY, BAKERLOO, CENTRAL AND VICTORIA LINES BENEFITED FROM UNEMPLOYMENT

**1921**    The government, alarmed by the rise in unemployment following the end of World War I and believing that the development would create 20,000 new jobs, underwrites a £6 million loan to create the Northern Line as far as Edgware.

**1929**    Ramsay Macdonald's government, underwrites a £13 million loan to extend the Piccadilly Line to Cockfosters and to reconstruct fifteen stations in central London, Piccadilly Circus station receiving the most spectacular makeover.

**1935**    Yet another unemployment scare prompts Neville Chamberlain to agree a £40 million programme to improve transport facilities in London which led to the extension of the Northern, Bakerloo and Central Lines.

**1952**    The London Transport Executive proposes the construction of the much-needed Victoria Line. However, the Treasury delays authorizing the expenditure.

**1962**    Ten years later London Transport management, knowing that the government is concerned about unemployment in the north-east as an election approaches, announces that the tunnel segments for the new line will be ordered from north-east shipyards. This piece of opportunism finally secures the finance.

# Underground Management

From the mid-1970s the financial problems of the London Underground made its management easy prey for politicians and journalists. Senior managers struggled to reconcile their public service obligations with the financial constraints imposed on them by their political masters, some of whom seemed intent on making their difficult job impossible. In 1978 Leslie Chapman, a former civil servant and author of a book on government waste (*Your Disobedient Servant*),was appointed to cut costs in London Transport. The *Evening Standard* announced the appointment under the headline 'The Axeman Cometh' with a picture of Chapman brandishing an axe. Although Chapman was subsequently dismissed at the insistence of the Underground chairman, Peter Masefield, this was the atmosphere in which the management had to operate. In the words of London Transport's then chief secretary, hard-working employees felt 'they were being branded as wasters and parasites'. Despite all this, both passenger numbers and productivity increased significantly under the chairmanship of Keith Bright as a result of good management and careful investment.

## AMAZING FACT

Leslie Chapman, appointed to cut costs at the Underground was dismissed after giving a particularly outrageous press interview.

## 'FARES FAIR'

One episode in the troubled financial history of the Underground was particularly acrimonious. In 1981 the Labour Party gained control of the

An attempt was made to discredit Keith Bright in a book by claiming that Bright drove an Aston Martin. However, the story was tarnished by the fact that he had bought the offending vehicle third-hand from his former employers.

Greater London Council. In October they introduced the 'Fares Fair' initiative, cutting fares by almost one third in an attempt to regain passengers for public transport but the hole thus created in the Underground's budget had to be plugged by the ratepayers of London to the tune of £125 million. The Conservative Borough of Bromley, which has no Underground stations, challenged the policy and in December 1981 the House of Lords judged in favour of the residents of Bromley. Fares were doubled, passengers numbers fell to below the level before 'Fares Fair' was introduced and, after a period of further mayhem, fares settled down at a level about twelve per cent higher than they had been at the start of the exercise: about enough to account for the inflation that had occurred in the meantime.

Unfortunately a change of political masters did not improve the relationship between the politicians and the management. In August 2000, shortly after being elected as the first Mayor of London, Ken Livingstone in a BBC interview described the Underground management team as 'not the brightest' and added, 'When I take over next April many of them will be heading for early retirement.'

## THE SOCIALIST AND THE CAPITALIST: UNIFICATION OF THE UNDERGROUND

Herbert Morrison, Labour Minister for Transport, and Albert Stanley, Lord Ashfield, were together responsible for the establishment in 1933 of the London Passenger Transport Board which unified the Underground as a single organization. Morrison introduced the necessary legislation whereby the Board was to assume control of all London bus and underground railway operations, including the Metropolitan Railway which had, to that point, remained independent of Lord Ashfield's Underground Group. Ashfield persuaded shareholders that the proposed arrangement offered by Morrison, being well short of outright nationalization, was the best they could hope for. Shareholders in The Underground Group and the Metropolitan Railway would receive interest-bearing stock in exchange for their shares, together with some cash for transfer of ownership. In this way an arm's-length relationship with government was maintained until full nationalisation in 1948 when the stockholders were bought out.

## FINANCING THE UNDERGROUND

Hopes that the London Underground could continue to be run by a public body while upgrades of stations, signalling, track and rolling stock could be undertaken by a Public Private Partnership (PPP) proved groundless when in 2005 London's Transport Commissioner, Bob Kiley, described the results of the PPP as 'Bordering on disaster'. The PPP operation was brought back into the control of Transport for London at a cost of over £2 billion.

**HERBERT MORRISON** (1888–1965)

- Born in Brixton, the son of a London policeman.

- Worked as a grocer's errand boy for seven shillings (35p) a week.

- Became active in local politics and in 1910 joined the Labour Party.

- Was MP for Hackney and a member of the London County Council (LCC), representing Woolwich.

- Became leader of the LCC in 1934 and was a member until 1945.

- Minister of Transport in 1929 and conceived the London Passenger Transport Board.

**DID YOU KNOW?**

Peter Mandelson is Herbert Morrison's grandson and continued the family association with the Labour Party.

The Metronet lines continue to be run by Transport for London but the company's financial problems do not auger well for the future of the network. It is to be hoped that ensuring appropriate investment in the network will not again be reliant on large-scale unemployment.

**ALBERT STANLEY, LORD ASHFIELD** (1874–1948)

- Born Albert Knatriess in Derby.

- Emigrated with his parents to the USA as a child.

- Aged 14, joined the Detroit Street Railway as a messenger boy.

- Family name changed to Stanley in 1897.

- At 29 he became General Manager of New Jersey Tramways.

- On insistence of American shareholders was appointed to keep an eye on George Gibb in Yerkes' *Underground Electric Railways of London.*

- Succeeded Gibb as General Manager in 1910.

- Resumed British citizenship, was knighted in 1914 and served as President of the Board of Trade.

- In 1920 became Lord Ashfield and served as chairman of the London Passenger Transport Board from its creation in 1933 and briefly served on its successor, the British Transport Commission, in the months before his death in 1948.

# Trains and Tunnels

The network is often referred to as 'The Tube' but strictly speaking the Metropolitan, District, Circle and Hammersmith & City lines are not deep-level tubes but sub-surface lines, just below street level, reached by stairs rather than by escalators or lifts. The City and South London Railway was the first deep-level railway. The first "tube" was the Tower Subway across the Thames just upstream from Tower Bridge. It was a cable operated railway, opened in 1870. It was not a commercial success and was soon adapted to convey water pipes and power cables beneath the Thames, as it still does.

## THE FIRST LOCOMOTIVES

When the Metropolitan Railway opened in 1863 it used steam engines specially designed by Daniel Gooch (1816-89), Brunel's former mechanical engineer on the Great Western. It was hoped that, by condensing the steam and returning it to the locomotive's water tank, the escape of steam into the tunnels would be minimised. The experiment was not altogether a success and besides, it did nothing about the smoke. Early accounts of Underground travel include evocative descriptions of the discomfort occasioned by the heat, smoke and noxious fumes while the noise of the train wheels on the steel rails in the confined space was compared with 'the shrieking of ten thousand demons'. When the Metropolitan District Railway opened between South Kensington and Westminster five years later and employing the same design, 'blow-holes' in the street were created to allow the fumes to escape.

**R.D.BLUMENFELD** (1864–1948)

- Born in Wisconsin, the son of German immigrants.

- Joined the *Chicago Herald* in 1884, visiting England to report Queen Victoria's Golden Jubilee in 1887.

- Spent most of the rest of his life in London.

- His diary provides an invaluable account of London at the turn of the century, with many references to London's Underground Railway and its shortcomings.

- Appointed editor of *The Daily Mail* in 1900 after a chance encounter in a barber's shop with Albert Harmsworth (Lord Northcliffe).

- Joined the rival *Daily Express* two years later.

- Introduced the banner headline (enlivened by often dreadful puns) into modern newspapers.

- In 1907 became a British citizen and later declined a knighthood.

# A SANATORIUM FOR ASTHMA AND BRONCHIAL COMPLAINTS

A Board of Trade Committee was formed to enquire into the problems caused by the fuming tunnels and was reassured by the manager of the Metropolitan Railway that the fumes were positively health-giving and that the particularly noxious Great Portland Street station was 'Actually used as a sanatorium for men who had been afflicted with asthma and bronchial complaints.' A Metropolitan Railway driver, Mr A.Langford, told the committee of his excellent health despite thirty-four years service in the tunnels. Unfortunately, he spoilt his evidence by adding that 'very seldom' was the smoke so thick as to render the signals invisible! It is not surprising that Robert Perks believed that electrification was the future.

---

### FIRST EXPERIENCE OF HADES

'I had my first experience of Hades to-day, and if the real thing is to be like that I shall never again do anything wrong. I got into the Underground Railway at Baker Street. I wanted to go to Moorgate Street...the smoke and the sulphur fill the tunnel, all the windows have to be closed. The atmosphere was a mixture of sulphur, coal dust and foul fumes from the gas lamps above; so that by the time we reached Moorgate Street I was near dead of asphyxiation and heat. I should think these Underground railways must soon be discontinued, for they are a menace to health'.
*From the diary of R. D. Blumenfeld, 1887*

---

### AMAZING FACT

Contemporary accounts tell of chemists selling a tonic called Metropolitan Mixture to revive fainting passengers.

**SIR JOHN ELLIOT** (1898-1988)

- Son of R D Blumenfeld.

- Followed his father into journalism and became assistant editor of the *Evening Standard* owned by Lord Beaverbrook.

- Changed his name to John Elliot in 1922 on Beaverbrook's advice because of post World War I anti-German prejudice.

- Fired by the whimsical Beaverbrook, in 1925 he joined the Southern Railway during the electrification period to improve its image through public relations and advertising.

- Soon moved to managing the railway itself and became Deputy General Manager.

- Ended his career as Chairman of London Transport and fought a long, bitter but eventually successful campaign for the construction of the Victoria Line.

# MARC BRUNEL AND THE TUNNELLING SHIELD

The construction of the deep-level Tube Railways, beginning with the City and South London Railway in 1890, would not have been possible without the invention of the Tunnelling Shield by Marc Brunel, based on his observation of the shipworm. He designed a rectangular frame, called a shield, 21 feet high and 36 feet wide. It was divided into 18 compartments on three levels, each level having six compartments containing one labourer with pick and shovel. The shield would be pressed up against the surface that was to be excavated and the labourers would set to, excavating the ground ahead of them, the spoil being removed by carts or by a moving belt behind them. When about 3 feet of earth had been excavated in this way the shield would be moved forward by screw jacks and the excavators began again, protected from falling debris by the shield itself. Bricklayers followed, lining the tunnel that had been created.

## EXTRAORDINARY FACT

Brunel's invention of the all-important tunnelling shield was inspired by the shipworm *teredo navalis* which ate into the wood of which ships were made. Its excrement formed a hard crust behind it which prevented the resultant tunnel from collapsing.

# TUNNELLING TECHNOLOGY

Tunnelling Technology advanced rapidly in the late nineteenth century, initially through the work of the civil engineer Peter William Barlow (1809-85). He developed a technique that was an advance on the tunnelling shield of Marc Brunel to build the Tower Subway. He had used cast-iron cylinders as piers for the original Lambeth suspension bridge and realised that, by turning them on their sides, he could form a tunnel beneath the river. In the Tower Subway this cylindrical shield was used to create a tunnel to hold iron segments which were bolted into place to form the subway. This idea of the cylindrical shield, a more robust and appropriate form than Brunel's rectangular model, was a major step forward in tunnelling technology. It was used later by the South African engineer James Greathead (1844-96) who had worked with Barlow on the Tower Subway to bore the tunnels for the City and South London Railway. He further developed the design to incorporate sharp steel blades which loosened the earth for the miners to excavate. Finally the English engineer John Price added electrically powered rotating blades which did most of the excavating work and this 'Price Rotary Excavator' was used to create the tunnels for Yerkes' Charing Cross, Euston and Hampstead Railway in the early years of the twentieth century.

**DID YOU KNOW?**

The twelve hundred foot long Thames Tunnel between Wapping and Rotherhithe was the first tunnel ever to be built beneath a river.

## The Tower Subway

The Tower Subway ran beneath the Thames from Tower Hill to Pickleherring Street (close to the present site of HMS

**HAPPIER MEMORIES OF THE UNDERGROUND TUNNELS**

'I have known a man, dying a long way from London, sigh queerly for the sight of a gush of smoke that, on a platform of the Underground, one may see escaping in great woolly clots'.

*The Soul of London* (1895) Ford Madox Ford

Belfast). It was opened in August 1870 and passengers paid a penny (second class) or two pence (first class) to be drawn by cable on narrow gauge carriages under the river. A stationary steam engine provided the power. Unfortunately, toll-free London Bridge was available nearby so few people used the subway and it never made a profit though it did survive as a foot tunnel without the cable railway.

### THE DUKE OF WELLINGTON'S PICKLED EELS

The Thames Tunnel was eventually opened by the Duke of Wellington. The occasion was marked by some notably unmemorable verse written for the occasion:

*The great big Duke of Wellington in splendour on does reel,*
*And through the tunnel he will go, to buy some pickled eels.*

This is the only record of the Iron Duke's devotion to the Cockney delicacy!

The tunnel, though visited by the royal family and commented upon by numerous foreign visitors, never made money and was eventually sold to the East London Railway, an often forgotten corner of the underground network.

When Tower Bridge opened in 1894 the Tower Subway closed. However, it has found another use and now conducts water and power lines beneath the river.

**DID YOU KNOW?**
The Channel Tunnel was built using the same technology as was used for the Tower Subway in 1870.

### SIR MARC BRUNEL (1769-1849)

- Father of Isambard Kingdom Brunel

- Born in France and learned mathematics from Gaspard Monge, secretary to the French navy.

- Fled to New York after the outbreak of the French Revolution, where he became the City Engineer, before going to England in 1799.

- Invented a mechanical process for making ships' blocks, enabling the Royal Navy to expand rapidly and destroy the French Navy.

- Responsible for many other inventions including a machine to make boots for Wellington's armies, a knitting machine and a typewriter.

- His business acumen did not match his inventiveness and he spent time in the King's Bench debtors' prison, from which he was rescued by a belated payment from the Admiralty of £5,000 for his block-maker.

# EARLY ELECTRICS: THE CITY AND SOUTH LONDON RAILWAY

The **City and South London Railway** opened in 1890 but, unlike the Metropolitan Railway, could not be powered by steam locomotives because it was too far beneath the surface for smoke and steam to escape through blow holes. The original proposal was to use a system invented by a Londoner called Andrew Hallidie and adopted by the cable cars of San Francisco. The trains would be pulled along by an endless cable which would be powered by steam engines at each end of the line, supplied with adequate ventilation. It was not clear how the system would ensure that the cable stopped at precisely the point at which the trains were positioned in the intermediate stations, bearing in mind that the same cable

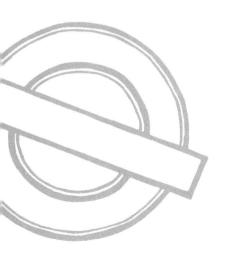

The Manchester firm of Mather and Platt designed a locomotive which would run at 25 mph on 450 volts, supplied by a power station at Stockwell. The locomotives hauled three carriages, known as 'padded cells' for their lush upholstery and small windows, the latter supposedly designed so that passengers would not be alarmed by the too-easily-visible sight of tunnel walls rushing past so far beneath the surface.

would pull trains in both directions; or how the operator would know that all the passengers were safely aboard before starting again. Nor was it explained how the cable would cope with the numerous bends on the City to Stockwell line. For these reasons the directors took the bold decision to adopt electric traction, a novel technology which a German called Magnus Volk had used in 1883 on a small railway on Brighton sea-front which is still in use.

# DEVELOPMENT OF ROLLING STOCK

On the City and South London Railway, for the first time there was no distinction between first and second class passengers which aroused the indignation of the ever-censorious *Railway Times*: *we have scarcely yet been educated up to that condition of social equality when lords and ladies will be content to ride side by side with Billingsgate 'fish fags' and Smithfield butchers.*

Passenger carriages on the early Metropolitan and the District were indistinguishable from those of surface railways. Tunnels were built accordingly which explains why there is still more headroom for rolling stock on these sub-surface lines (Metropolitan, District, Circle and Hammersmith & City) than on the 'tubes'. The padded cells of the City and South London Railway were the first to have a distinctively 'underground' character, and they were followed by the 'Gatestock' carriages of the Central London Railway. Passengers joined and alighted from the train through gates at one end of each carriage. Each carriage had a 'gateman' who would check that all passengers were safely aboard before enacting an elaborate system of hand signals to indicate to the driver and guard that it was safe to depart. 'Gatestock' trains were expensive to operate because of the staff required. The Gatestock survived on the Bakerloo Line until 1930. In 1919 air-operated sliding doors were introduced, after which

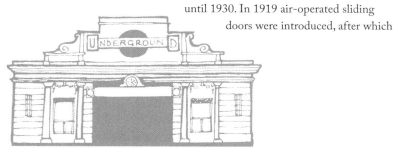

only three crew members were required: a driver and guard at the front of the train and a rear guard who operated the doors. These carriages required no locomotive since the electric motor was situated behind the driver's cab where it occupied a considerable space which would have been better devoted to passengers. However, by 1938 advances

in design and technology made it possible for the motors to be suspended beneath the carriages, thus releasing more room for passengers. Because of its robustness, this design was introduced to the Isle of Wight Railway thirty years later. The concept, maximising passenger space, still underpins Underground rolling stock design.

The locomotives of the Central London Railway were much heavier and more powerful and were bought from the General Electric company of the USA (still a leading manufacturer of locomotives). The effect of the 43-ton monsters on the draughtsmen in offices above has already been noted in the entry on the Central Line.

# The Underground at War

The tunnels of the Underground network played a vital role in providing shelter for the hundreds of thousands of Londoners seeking safety from bombing raids. The use of the stations was a fine example of 'power of the people', but the experience was far from pleasant. Although camaraderie was undoubtedly strong, conditions were truly rank: lice travelled from person to person with ease while swarms of mostquitoes invaded the warm, moist tunnels, attracted by the stench from people relieving themselves in the tunnels.

## WOMEN JOIN THE WORK-FORCE

During World War I the Underground railways lost between one third and one half of their staff to military service and companies started to employ women at stations. The *Railway Gazette*, whose editor was noted for his disapproving attitude to anything that could be described as progressive, grumpily conceded that this development was 'preferable to employing hobbledehoys'. By 1917 women were replacing gatemen on trains though drivers and guards were exclusively male. The women's heavy serge uniforms were not designed to be alluring and the employment of women in these roles did not long survive the war's end.

**DID YOU KNOW?**

Maida Vale station was the first to be run exclusively by women, a male stationmaster being shared with three neighbouring stations. The owners had agreed with the trade unions not only that women should be employed but also, half a century before the Equal Pay Act, that they would receive the same pay as men.

## TUNNELS USED AS AIR-RAID SHELTERS

The comparatively modest air raids of World War I prompted Londoners to seek refuge in the tube stations. As many as 300,000 sought refuge in February 1918, almost twice the number recorded for World War II. In World War II it was believed that deaths from bombing would be so great that the network would be required to shift a daily toll of 10,000 corpses. In addition it was feared that other citizens, terrified by air raids, would take up a subterranean existence and refuse to emerge from their underground refuges, with disastrous consequences for the war effort.

## LONDONERS DECIDE HOW THE TUBE STATIONS ARE TO BE USED

If the government had had its way no-one would have sheltered in the tubes in the World War II. A notice was published stating:

> The public are informed that, in order to operate the railways for essential movement, Underground stations cannot be used as air raid shelters

The public decided otherwise. On the evening of 8th September 1940, as the Blitz gathered pace, a large group of determined citizens forced their way into Liverpool Street Underground station, pushing aside the hapless police, Underground employees and Home Guard volunteers who were supposed to stop them. In the words of *Picture Post*, 'London decided how the tube stations were to be used'. The government recognized a *fait accompli* when it saw one. From that date the tubes were available to anyone who wanted to shelter in them, an arrangement that continued throughout the Blitz and was revived with the arrival of V-weapons in 1944.

## TAKING SHELTER

All deep-level tube stations were eventually opened as shelters along with a number of disused and partly-built stations and tunnels. These included the Aldwych branch which was closed during the war; the disused King William Street to Borough branch of the City and South London Railway; and the disused station at British Museum. Lavatories were installed in shelters and a ticketing system introduced, season tickets being issued to regular users engaged on important work or with family responsibilities. Harmony was not always achieved, the following verbal exchange being initiated in one shelter by a lady whose bed was close to the lavatory:

36 doctors and 20 nurses set up medical posts in the shelters to provide free care for the sick (eight years before the National Health Service was created) and many babies entered the world in tube shelters.

*'Seventy-eight people want to go to the lavatory'.*
*'Can't you shut up, you bleeding little hypocrite?'*
*'I want to go to sleep and these people keep on going
to the lavatory'.*

## THE BLITZ SPIRIT

People seeking shelter were admitted from 4 pm and individual stations became communities with libraries, films, music and even live theatrical productions. An attempt to introduce classical music on gramophone records was not well received; the listeners complained that the noise of the music made it impossible to hear the falling bombs! Classes in dressmaking were well attended while chess, dominoes and darts proved popular, an inter-shelter darts league being particularly well supported. On one occasion, the sound of a piano, ingeniously transported from a nearby pub, was added to that of mouth organs and banjos played by amateur musicians. Raffles were held to buy Christmas presents for children, eleven thousand being distributed at Christmas 1940. Some tube shelters produced newspapers with titles like *De Profundis* ('from the depths'), the Latin title presumably indicating the classical education of its Swiss Cottage residents.

AMAZING FACT

In one station George Formby, precariously seated on a platform above the track, played his ukulele to the shelterers.

TO THE TRAINS

# LIFE UNDERGROUND

By providing a reasonably safe and often quiet environment, the tube shelters made it possible for Londoners to have a good night's sleep to prepare them for their daily work, much of it vital for the war effort. Most were regular users and settled down to games of cards and dominoes, small wagers being settled by the exchange of food and cigarettes. Children were, with difficulty, persuaded to go to sleep in exchange for bribes in the form of sweets and occasionally a few people would venture to the surface to bring back reports of the carnage on the streets. Sleep averaged three to five hours a night, women sleeping less than men on account of their care of the children. When the raids ended with Hitler's invasion of Russia in the spring of 1941 the stations soon emptied though they came into use again in 1944 with the arrival of the 'Doodlebugs' and V2 rockets.

## VISITORS

Leonard and Virginia Woolf visited the tube shelter at Russell Square and Leonard described 'dozens of men, women and children on mattresses wrapped in sheets and blankets and lying side by side down the platform as if they were sardines in a giant tin.' Not all visitors were welcome. The writer Constantine Fitzgibbon explained:

*Some people from the West End who used to go sightseeing to shelters, just as before the war they would make up jolly parties to visit Chinatown. Needless to say slumming of this sort was not at all popular with the shelterers and at least one party of sightseers was roughly ejected.*

George Orwell wrote: 'Foreigners are more frightened than English people during the raids. It is not their war and therefore they have nothing to sustain them'. But he also commented favourably on the civility that prevailed in the shelters and on their 'cleanly, normal, domesticated air.'

## INTO BATTLE

Two Underground stations played a particularly critical role during the bombardments of World War II. The disused Brompton Road station, became the control centre for the anti-aircraft batteries that protected London. Leicester Square station, very much in use, assumed an important role in the defence against V2 rockets. It was feared that one would land in the Thames, penetrate one of the tubes beneath the river and flood the network, causing catastrophic casualties. Ground radar was directed at the launch V2 sites and as soon as it appeared that London was the target for a rocket, a control centre at Leicester Square was warned by telephone. The control centre then had four minutes to clear trains through the tunnels and close floodgates on either side of the Thames, to seal off the tunnels and prevent flooding. Many trains were delayed in this way without the passengers knowing the true reason. No catastrophic strike ever occurred but the precaution was wise.

**EXTRAORDINARY FACT**
Three-tier bunks were installed in some stations to accommodate 22,000 people (out of a total of 150,000 at the height of the Blitz) but the bunks were actually removed from two stations when some of the more high-spirited residents complained that they left no room for dancing!

**DID YOU KNOW?**

Despite what the public thought, the underground stations and tunnels were not immune to the bombs. The worst incident came on the night of 14 October 1940 when some 600 people were sheltering in Balham station, 30 feet (about 9m) beneath Balham High Road, when a direct hit burst the water main directly above and flooded the station. Those not killed by the blast and falling rubble were drowned.

The maintenance depot at Aldenham, in Hertfordshire, became an aircraft factory where 710 Halifax bombers were assembled. And at the Acton rolling-stock maintenance depot, Sherman tanks were converted to 'Swimming Tanks' which accompanied troops landing on the beaches during the invasion of Normandy. Their use significantly reduced casualties compared with those sustained on the American beaches which did not use them. At Earl's Court station the subway which led to the exhibition hall was converted into an aircraft component factory, the labour being provided by London Transport employees who worked on after the ends of their shifts.

For some years before the war the management of the Underground had been concerned about the disappearance of the rubber grips suspended from the ceilings of carriages for the use of passengers who had no seat. It was thought that they were being used as coshes by gangsters. They were cast in a more heroic light after the battle of El Alamein in 1942 when the British Eighth Army occupied Algeria. Ever alert to a good story, London Transport's publicity department announced that one had been found in the streets of Algiers, supposedly left there earlier following a raid by the Special Air Service (SAS). Was this true? How else could it have got there? It's certainly a good story.

# STRANGE STRUCTURES

As the Blitz drove Londoners into underground stations and other air raid shelters, the Home Secretary announced that 'a new system of tunnels linked to the London tubes' would be bored. Eight were eventually completed in 1942 and it was believed at the time that they would be used to house government agencies if Hitler unleashed 'terror weapons' preventing government from functioning above ground. Each was capable of sleeping 8,000 people. Seven were built alongside existing Northern Line stations, prompting speculation that, after the war, they would be linked in a continuous tunnel to relieve the terribly overcrowded Northern Line trains, like the New York 'Rapid Transit' system where a fast tube line runs alongside the conventional metro lines. Each shelter had a diameter of 16 feet 6 inches, about one and a half times that of the normal tubes, supporting the theory that they were designed to accommodate express trains eventually. If that was the plan, it was never implemented and the Northern Line remains the most overcrowded on the network. The eighth shelter is near Chancery Lane station and became a telephone exchange.

The new shelter in Chenies Street, near Goodge Street station, was used by Generals Eisenhower and Montgomery for the initial planning of the D-Day invasions and later became the communications HQ for the British and Canadian beaches Gold, Juno and Sword. The first accounts of the drama unfolding on the Normandy beaches were received here. This shelter is now The Eisenhower Centre and, like the other 'Northern Line' shelters, is used as a document store. The Clapham Common shelter also played a part in a corner of British history. When the Empire Windrush arrived with the first West Indian immigrants in June 1948, the shelter was used to house the new arrivals. From there, they made their way in search of work to the nearby Labour Exchange in Coldharbour Lane, Brixton. Thus was born Brixton's Afro-Caribbean community.

# THE WORLD'S LONGEST FACTORY

At the outbreak of World War II the Central Line extensions to Leytonstone, Hainault and Epping were well advanced. Most of the tunnelling had been completed but the track and signals had not yet been laid. It was decided therefore to use the tunnels to create the world's longest factory for the manufacture of components for Churchill tanks, Spitfires and Lancaster and Halifax bombers. The elongated shape of the factory prompted the installation of a narrow gauge track to move raw materials and components along the production lines. At the end of the war, when construction of the Central Line extension resumed, the factory was relocated to nearby Ilford and eventually purchased by Siemens.

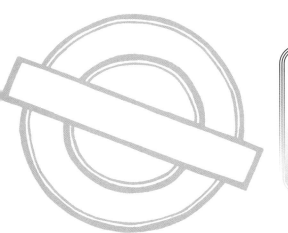

## THE MOST HATED PASSENGER

One of the Underground's less admired contributions to the war effort was *Billy Brown*, whose sanctimonious homilies were delivered to passengers in a series of cartoons on posters. They were the brainchild of a cartoonist called David Langdon whose hero urged passenger to behave like frantic boy scouts and perform a good deed each day. One rhyme advised:

> To-day's Good Deed
> When you travel to and fro
> On a line you really know,
> Remember those who aren't so sure
> And haven't been that way before.
> Do your good deed for the day
> Tell them the stations on the way

The imagination struggles with the image of hapless passengers being hunted down and thus instructed by Billy's followers, if he had any. Another account had Billy being commended by magistrates for preventing a passenger from lighting up in a 'no smoking' carriage though the means he employed was not specified. *The Daily Mail* probably spoke for many when it threatened:

> Some day very soon, by heck,
> Billy Brown, I'll wring your neck.

After that, Billy passed into history, unmourned.

# Underground Art, Architecture, Poetry and Maths

In addition to its involvement in Britain's political and social history, the Underground made (and continues to make) an important contribution to many aspects of British life, as well as to commuters' daily experience. Innovative developments in the Underground and cutting-edge creativity are evident, for example, in the design and materials employed in stations and in the famous London Underground posters.

## HARRY BECK'S MAP

In 1931 Harry Beck was sitting at home having been made redundant by the Underground Group during one of its recurrent financial crises. He began to sketch a diagram of the Underground Railway network, following principles of design familiar to him as an electrical draughtsman. First, he used the Central Line as a horizontal axis around which to build the map. Secondly, where lines intersected he used mainly 45 and 90 degree angles. Thirdly, he used colours to distinguish the lines. Finally, the distance between the stations as they appeared on his map bore no resemblance to the true distance on the ground. He reasoned that passengers were concerned only that they were travelling in the right direction on the right line and had no interest in the distances involved. Thus he was able to accommodate the whole network on one poster of manageable size. He submitted the idea to a publicity committee headed by the company's vice-chairman, Frank Pick, but the proposal was rejected. The following year, the committee reconsidered the proposal and decided to try it out with a small print-run. All the copies were taken up by the public within a month and Pick confessed, 'This looks very convenient and tidy and is a better map than any we have had so far.' Harry Beck's map remains the supreme example of twentieth century graphic design: simple, clear, attractive and supremely good at its job of helping people to find their way around London. Instantly recognizable, it is printed under licence on clothing, mousemats, book jackets and aprons.

Frank Pick was possibly the most influential person in the history of the London Underground. Born in Lincolnshire, into a Quaker family, he qualified as a solicitor before joining the North-Eastern Railway. He moved to the Underground Group as part of the team that George Gibb brought with him in 1905 when he accepted Sir Edgar Speyer's invitation to rescue the network from the financial machinations of Charles Tyson Yerkes. He was soon given the task by Albert Stanley of sorting out the company's marketing and publicity. Pick eventually became vice-chairman of the company. A cold and sometimes severe man, he made unannounced visits to stations, depots and other installations to check that all was as he wished and, when it wasn't, withering letters in his dreaded green ink would follow. Pick became a founding member of the Design and Industries Association and later Chairman of a forerunner of the Design Council.

# DESIGN AND INDUSTRIES ASSOCIATION GONE MAD

Frank Pick asked Charles Holden to design stations for the Morden extension of the Northern Line and Holden's designs prompted an uncharacteristically excited Pick to write: We are going to build our stations upon the Morden extension railway to the most modern pattern. We are going to discard entirely all ornament. We are going to represent the Design and Industries Association gone mad.

**CHARLES HOLDEN (1875-1960)**

- The most important architect in the history of the London Underground.

- Believed that architecture should "throw off its mantle of deceits, its cornices, pilasters, mouldings".

- Spent his childhood in Bolton in straitened circumstances, his mother having died when he was eight and his father's business having gone bankrupt.

- Worked initially as a railway clerk until his brother-in-law arranged for him to be apprenticed to a Manchester architect.

- One of his earliest designs was for Bristol Central Library.

- In 1897 began to practice in London and designed the HQ for the British Medical Association in the Strand (now Zimbabwe House), incorporating sculpture by Jacob Epstein.

These principles are particularly evident in the station at Clapham Common, a simple geometric design clad in Portland Stone, similar to others on the line and, like many of them, a listed building. Holden's next task was to redesign Piccadilly Circus station. The cramped booking hall at ground level at the foot of Regent Street was grossly overcrowded but could not be extended. Holden's solution was to build a new booking hall beneath Eros. While this was in construction, Holden and Pick were preparing for the even greater challenge of designing stations for the extensions of the Central and Piccadilly Lines. In 1930 Holden joined Pick on his *Who's Who* listed hobby of 'visiting and studying the transport systems of other countries', travelling to Germany, the Netherlands and Sweden. On their return they wrote a paper stating their firm belief that "fitness for purpose is a necessary attribute of all good design" and arguing that new materials and techniques like reinforced concrete, steel frames and plate glass offered opportunities to innovate in a way not seen since the middle ages.

Frank Pick commissioned the architect Charles Holden to design stations on the Northern, Piccadilly and Central Line extensions. The result was a series of ground-breaking designs, using modern materials and ideas, taken from the Bauhaus and using simple geometric forms. Many of these are now listed buildings, notably the station at Arnos Grove on the Piccadilly Line.

## AMAZING FACT

As World War II approached, the Women's Voluntary Service wanted a poster to recruit more women for their relief work. Pick was approached and asked his assistant to find a young woman, resolute-looking and attractive but not too glamorous, to be the model. This task completed, the posters were printed and the necessary recruits found. The press enquired as to the identity of the young woman. She turned out to be German, a fact that was successfully concealed for over 50 years.

# THE HOLDEN AND PICK LEGACY

Holden and Pick were responsible for a chain of listed buildings for the Piccadilly and Central Lines. But Holden did not just concern himself with buildings: he also ensured that lighting, platform seats, kiosks, ticket machines and litter bins were integrated into a harmonious whole. He designed the Underground headquarters,

## FRANK PICK VERSUS WINSTON CHURCHILL

Pick was asked to advise on the design of leaflets to be dropped over Germany during the phoney war of 1940. However, he objected to the dropping of leaflets containing false news and was summoned to see Churchill. The following conversation ensued.

**CHURCHILL:** Now Mr Pick, I understand you have been objecting to the dropping of the leaflets.

**PICK:** Yes, Prime Minister, what is written on the leaflets is not wholly true and that is bad propaganda.

**CHURCHILL:** This is no time to be concerned with the niceties.

**PICK:** Prime Minister, I have never told a lie in my life.

**CHURCHILL:** Mr Pick, yesterday the Germans shelled Dover with their long-range guns at Cape Gris Nez. This afternoon I shall be visiting Dover. I may be killed by a German shell. If so, it will be a great comfort to me to know that on the last day of my life I spoke with a man who had never told a lie in his life. Get out.

That was Frank Pick's last contribution to the war effort and he died the following year. He had refused both a knighthood and a peerage.

the tallest office building in London when it opened in 1929. Of cruciform shape in granite and Portland stone, it makes generous use of glass to maximize light. The exterior of the building incorporated sculptures by Henry Moore, Eric Gill and Jacob Epstein. *The Times* applauded the use of Eric Gill's designs as "a serious attempt – almost the first that has been made in this country – to employ first-rate sculptors to decorate and complete a building". Charles Holden died in 1960, having refused a knighthood on the grounds that architecture involved too much teamwork to justify the award of an honour to one person.

## AMAZING FACT

One of Holden's most neglected designs is Gants Hill station. The magnificent concourse is believed to owe much to Moscow's grand *Pushkinskaya* station.

Frank Pick is remembered for his commitment to high quality design in station architecture, and in posters too. He befriended the artists Walter Gropius and Edward McKnight Kauffer. Gropius, who fled to England from Germany in the 1930s, brought Bauhaus ideas to England while Kauffer impressed Pick with his determination to make commercial poster design a serious art form. He became the Underground's principal designer of posters and formed *Group X* with the writer and artist Wyndham Lewis, who also designed posters for the Underground. They became leading members of the avant-garde movement in London and the impact of their work upon millions of commuters was acknowledged by Pevsner.

## ARCHITECTURAL IMPORTANCE OF UNDERGROUND STATIONS

Holden and Pick's station at Arnos Grove featured in Pevsner's *Outline of European Architecture*, with the comment that such examples of modern design 'helped more than anything to pave the way for the twentieth century style in England.'

# TRAFFIC ALL DAY LONG

In April 1909 Albert Stanley succeeded George Gibb as General Manager of the Underground Group. He knew that, to earn sufficient revenue the Underground needed 'traffic all day long and not just at the tidal movements of business'. So he gave Frank Pick responsibility for developing new services and publicising existing ones. He began by clearing up the clutter of miscellaneous machinery and advertising posters that sprawled over Underground stations, to the extent that passengers complained that they could not see station names! He laid down some ground rules for advertising; certain areas in stations were set aside for the route maps; and the famous 'Bar and Circle' design was introduced to highlight station names. Commercial advertising was confined to passages and designated parts of platforms and poster sites were of a standard size.

## HOW TO GET THERE

A board game called *How to Get There* was produced to get people familiar with the Underground. Like *Monopoly* (which came later), it required players to move trains round stations on a board overcoming obstacles such as 'Stop' signals and lost tickets. The press made merry with the game, suggesting such additions as 'Breakdown on District – return on foot'; 'Lift sticks on Central, lose six turns' and 'Polite conductor on Hampstead Tube – miss eight moves through shock'. The game was popular enough to run into a second edition.

## AMAZING FACT

The origin of the Underground's famous "Bar and Circle" design is uncertain but may have resulted from Albert Stanley seeing the rather similar Metro symbol on a visit to Paris.

# UNDERGROUND POSTERS: AN IMPORTANT ART FORM

Pick had seen how effectively the North-Eastern Railway (his previous employers) had used posters to promote travel to resorts like Scarborough . He also believed that, 'a poster must awaken a purpose in the mind' so every effort was made to identify destinations and events which would persuade passengers to travel. The Oxford and Cambridge Boat Race, museums, art

**DID YOU KNOW?**

Novelist Len Deighton is one of many famous people who have designed posters for the Underground (see below).

IN LONDON'S COUNTRY there are still many villages, described in Domesday, whose beauty survives. Here cottages crouch round the green or follow the line of the road as casually as the trees.

The Londoner should often see these quiet places as an antidote to his crowded streets.

The visitor from abroad cannot claim to have really seen London if he has neglected London's country and has not seen its villages. They offer a rewarding and a revealing sample of the essential England.

*London Transport's green Country Buses link these villages with Green Line coaches and the Underground. Write to the Public Relations Officer, 55 Broadway, S.W.1 for a free leaflet 'Village Life' that describes a dozen of the prettiest villages near London and shows you how to get there, or set out to make your own discoveries.*

galleries, theatres, air displays and shopping were amongst the many reasons given for underground travel. To ensure that the poster designs were of high quality Pick commissioned established artists like John Hassall as well as setting some younger artists on the road to success. These included Mabel Lucie Attwell, Rex Whistler, Paul Nash and Graham Sutherland.

**DID YOU KNOW?**

A competition to create an advertising slogan for the Underground was won by a 14-year old boy, Edward Parrington. The winning slogan 'Underground to Anywhere; Quickest Way, Cheapest Fare' gained him the prize of £10.

## POETRY ON THE UNDERGROUND

In 1986 poetry became and remains a familiar sight on Underground trains and posters. Featuring the work of poets, both living and deceased, well-known and less so, it brings poetry to three million people every day. The poems are chosen on their merits by a small group, including Judith Chernaik, the poet whose idea it was. In 2000 the Sydney Olympics led to *Australian Poetry on the Underground* and the work of several American poets has also been featured.

## MATHS ON THE UNDERGROUND

In the year 2000, *World Mathematical Year*, twelve posters were designed to be displayed month by month on the Underground. They included *Maths is cool* using a picture of a melting iceberg to illustrate catastrophe theory and *Maths takes off* to explain the principles of aerodynamics.

Poetry and Maths were not amongst the ideas adopted by Frank Pick but he would surely have approved.

> Many of the poems so far published may be seen on the Transport for London website and ten editions of the book *Poems on the Underground* have been published to date. One edition sold more than a quarter of a million copies.

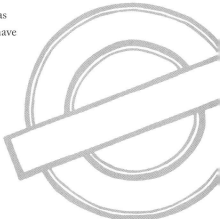

# Metroland and its Family

The Metropolitan Railway was successful in the field of property development (Metropolitan Country Estates Ltd) and coined the name *Metro-Land* (with a hyphen) in 1915 to promote suburban living and the long-distance commuting which promised higher revenues from fares. The name was popularised by John Betjeman in his poetry and by Evelyn Waugh whose Margot Metroland was a prominent character in his early works.

## THE METROPOLITAN RAILWAY AND PROPERTY

### The Watkin Tower

This spectacular failure, this was inspired by Sir Edward Watkin's visit to Paris and his conviction that a tower, built adjacent to his Metropolitan railway at Neasden, would attract crowds comparable to those that visited the Eiffel Tower. This would generate traffic for the railway as well as revenue for the tower itself which would, of course, be higher than the Eiffel Tower. In the event, the Neasden magistrates turned down an application for a licence to sell alcohol and the opening of the first stage of the tower attracted little notice, even locally. The restaurants, tea dances and Turkish bath attracted few people in the first year instead of the hordes confidently predicted by Watkin. The unloved fragment was blown up in 1907 and soon replaced by Wembley Stadium which did realize Watkin's dream of drawing passengers to the Metropolitan Railway.

> **EXTRAORDINARY FACT**
> Edward Watkin tried to persuade Gustave Eiffel to supervise the construction of the Watkin Tower at Neasden. He did not succeed.

## A Model Garden Village Where Peace and Quiet Prevail

Other less spectacular developments than the Watkin Tower were more successful. Kingsbury Garden Village, also in Neasden, was described by estate agents as:

> Great was our joy, Ronald Hughes Wright's and mine,
> To travel by the Underground all day
> Between the rush hours, so that very soon
> There was no station, north to Finsbury Park,
> To Barking eastwards, Clapham Common south,
> No temporary platform in the west
> Among the Actons and the Ealings, where
> We had not once alighted. Metroland
> Beckoned us out to lanes in beechy Bucks.
>
> (John Betjeman, from *Summoned by Bells*)

*A model garden village, on which a number of semi-detached residences have been erected. Peace and quiet prevail and the stretches of country around offer plenty of opportunity for invigorating exercise to those who are inclined to walking and cycling.*

Between 1901 and 1937 the population of inner London fell by almost half a million while that of Metroland and its sisters grew by two and a half million. The community most obviously affected by the opening of the Underground extensions was the village of Morden in Surrey at the southern extremity of the Northern Line. At the beginning of the twentieth century it had a population of 960. After Morden station opened in 1926, the population rose to 12,618 by 1931. The vision of Charles Pearson, who wanted to move workers from the slums of Smithfield to healthier

**AMAZING FACT**

The Metropolitan Railway made much more money from its property arm than it ever did from running trains.

# Metroland

**DID YOU KNOW?**

Evelyn Waugh was brought up in Metroland and his father took the Underground to work every day. He himself used Metroland as a source for some of his richest comic characters but he probably wouldn't want to be remembered as a member of one of the Underground's first commuter families.

residences in the fields that surrounded London in the 1850s had been realised, though not in the way he had foreseen.

## Metroland architects & architecture

Most of the buildings associated with Metroland were conventional terraced, semi-detached or detached houses but there was some architecture of distinction. Charles Voysey (1857-1941) the Arts and Crafts architect built *The Orchard* for himself in Chorleywood which remains a fine example of his characteristic style with its huge, steep-pitched gabled roofs, roughcast walls, leaded windows and specially designed furniture. Amersham in Buckinghamshire at the end of the Metropolitan Line acquired some fine houses of modern design but the most celebrated building was, in a sense, the headquarters of Metroland. This was Chiltern Court above the Metropolitan's Baker Street station, a development of half a million square feet of luxury flats, offices and retail units. Some of the flats contained ten bedrooms while other 'Bachelor Flats' had three bedrooms and thirty small bedrooms for maids were included. Early residents included the authors

## AMAZING FACT

Metropolitan Country Estates Ltd used popular songs with titles like 'My Little Metroland Home' or 'Neath the Shade of the Ruislip Poplars' to promote the sale of their suburban houses, the latter ending with this strained rhyming couplet:

*It's a very short distance by rail on the Met,*
*And at the gate you'll find waiting sweet Violet.*

Arnold Bennett and H.G. Wells and the Underground poster artist E. McKnight Kauffer. Harrods, after some hesitation, turned down the opportunity to take space on three floors and was quickly replaced by smaller outlets. In November 1929 the Chiltern Court Restaurant opened on the ground floor, seating 250 diners who would be serenaded from the musicians' gallery. The rental income from Chiltern Court of £40,000 a year on an investment of £500,000 (7.5%) was a better return than the Metropolitan could earn by running trains.

The Underground extensions that were built were not always welcomed. In 1924 the Northern Line reached Edgware and the railway urged inhabitants of the inner suburbs to move to the new terminus in the 'beautiful garden suburb, on a hillside facing south, protected from north winds and catching every gleam of sunshine.' The new community thrived and quickly reached a population of 13,000. The new commuters from Edgware and Highgate did not go down well with the residents of Hampstead, one of whom complained in a letter to *The Times* that 'the intelligentsia of Hampstead has the chagrin of witnessing the *canaille* of Highgate lolling at their ease while we have to hang on our straps. Is it fair?'

# Metroland

## STRAPHANGERS

The trains were often overcrowded and the consequences for some commuters were spelt out in a litany of complaining letters to newspapers in the 1930s. One asserted that during the evening peak on the Northern Line standing passengers were 'not less than sixty in every compartment. The discomfort is extreme, the air vitiated, everyone fatigued'. Another, who had the misfortune to travel on the busy Central Line, described the challenges presented to anyone wanting to board a second train, having failed at the first attempt:

*On several occasions I have been one of a bunch of rejects and have had to wait for another train. At such times one's only chance of adding to the crush inside was to judge the speed of approach and jockey for a position near a door. Once there I admit things are much easier; one only has to adopt a passive stance and a wave of surging humanity does the rest.*

Sir Edgar Speyer, however, told his shareholders that 'straphangers meant dividends.'

EXTRAORDINARY FACT

Some passengers went on strike. In April 1937 an Edgware-bound train was terminated at Colindale for some operational reason and the passengers were instructed to leave the train and board one which was following. Previous experience *suggested* to some of these seasoned travellers that the following train, if it existed, would be long delayed. So some of them stayed put and were duly shunted into a siding. A few moments later the promised train arrived and was boarded by the more timid passengers from the terminated train who were thus able to wave cheerily to the awkward squad as they sat glumly in their siding.

## Blessings have been showered upon your undertaking

Others were more appreciative. In 1922 Frank Pick began a campaign to extend the Piccadilly Line beyond Finsbury Park into the suburbs to Cockfosters in search of lucrative long-distance commuters. The plan was opposed by the London & North-Eastern Railway (LNER) which picked up passengers at Finsbury Park and carried them itself and was reluctant to lose the traffic. However the interchange between the Underground and the LNER at Finsbury Park was a scene of mayhem involving fights, nervous collapses and promising terrain for pickpockets. Pick arranged for photographs of the pandemonium to be taken from nearby buildings and these he distributed to newspapers and local MPs who used them to good effect in over-ruling the LNER's objections. Following the opening of the Piccadilly Line as far as Arnos Grove in September 1932, Pick received a letter from the local Federation of Ratepayers which read, 'Blessings have been showered upon your undertaking by thousands during the past month.'

> One possible remedy for overcrowding was put forward by one M. du Plat Taylor who wrote to *The Times* to suggest that the situation would be eased by the installation of parcel racks. He did not make clear whether they would be for parcels or for prostrate passengers but since he wrote from the exclusive London Club the Athenaeum he probably travelled by limousine anyway.

So it wasn't all bad.

# Accidents and Tragedies

The Underground has accommodated both fictional murders and the grimmer kind, as well as being the scene of terrible tragedy. Emma Magdalena Rosalia Maria Josefa Barbara Orczy, better known as Baroness Orczy (1865-1947) is remembered as the author of *The Scarlet Pimpernel* which she claimed to have conceived while queuing for a ticket at Tower Hill station (presumably the queue was a long one). She also wrote *The Mysterious Death on the Underground Railway* whose plot depended upon the fact that, following the opening of the Central London Railway in 1900, the carriages of the Metropolitan were often empty. A young woman is found dead in a carriage at Aldgate station and the absence of other passengers helps to ensure that the culprit escapes justice.

## MURDER ON THE UNDERGROUND

Countess Teresa Lubienska was a descendant of Polish landowners and had survived incarceration in Ravensbruck concentration camp before settling in Kensington where she was a respected member of the area's large Polish community. On the evening of 25th May 1957, she was stabbed to death at Gloucester Road station in an apparently motiveless murder. The murderer was never identified. On 13th July 1959 Gunther Fritz Podola, a petty criminal born in Berlin in 1929, was arrested by two policemen at a telephone booth at South Kensington station while making a call in which he was trying to blackmail a housewife. Podola produced a gun and shot dead Detective Sergeant Raymond Purdy, a married officer with three children. Podola was tried, found guilty and hanged on 5th November 1959, the last person to be executed for murdering a policeman. At Holborn station on 9th December 1988 a tourist was stabbed to death by a mugger who was subsequently arrested and convicted.

# TERRORISM

On 15th March 1976 Vincent Kelly, an Irish terrorist, carried a bomb on to a District Line train at Stepney Green station, intending to detonate it at Liverpool Street as the rush hour gathered pace. However he boarded the wrong train, heading out of town, and panicked when the bomb began to give off smoke at West Ham. He threw it down the carriage where it exploded, injuring nine other passengers as well as Kelly himself. Kelly then fled and was pursued by the driver, Stephen Julius, a married man who had come to London from the West Indies where London Transport was recruiting staff. Cornered, Kelly shot Stephen Julius dead, injured a post office engineer with another shot and tried to shoot himself. The worst attack on the London Underground occurred on 7th July 2005 when four suicide bombers mounted simultaneous attacks on underground trains near Liverpool Street, Edgware Road and Russell Square stations at 8.50 am, the height of the morning peak, an attack on a bus in Tavistock Square following an hour later. Fifty-six people died, including the four bombers. Two weeks later, on 21st July, four other would-be suicide bombers made bungled attempts at a similar operation which failed, all four being arrested and later sentenced to 40 years in prison.

## WARTIME TRAGEDIES

On the evening of 3rd March 1943, an orderly queue formed at Bethnal Green station on the Central Line to seek shelter from one of the bombing raids that occurred sporadically two years after the Blitz itself had ended. The exact cause of the tragic events that followed was never fully identified but may have been prompted

by some anti-aircraft gunfire from a battery in nearby Victoria Park being mistaken for an exploding bomb. Whatever the reason, the crowd surged forward on the stairway leading to the booking hall beneath the street and a young mother, with a baby, lost her footing and fell down the steps. In the panic that followed the young woman survived but 173 people died from crushing or suffocation. This was the worst civilian disaster of the Second World War and was for a time kept from the public.

On 12th October 1940 seven people were killed while sheltering in Trafalgar Square station (now incorporated in Charing Cross station) when a bomb penetrated Whitehall. Two nights later nineteen were killed at Bounds Green station on the Piccadilly Line. Sixteen of the dead were Belgians who had fled their country at the time of Dunkirk, four months earlier, and had set up a temporary home on the station platform. The other three were local residents who had been bombed out of their home on a previous raid and had been welcomed to the little Belgian colony. The reaction of one elderly lady typified the phlegmatic attitude of many at that difficult time. Viewing the scene of the tragedy she commented, 'We'll sleep well tonight. At least there'll be no trains coming through.' In January 1941 a bomb fell on the roadway above the busy Bank station, penetrating to the platforms beneath and exploding as a train entered the station. The driver was blown from his seat and the train ran down passengers who had been blasted into its path, fifty-six being killed.

# Accidents and Tragedies

## THE MOORGATE DISASTER

Leslie Newson was a man of quiet life and sober habits. A veteran of Dunkirk, he was accepted for training as a guard on the London Underground in 1969 and in 1974 he became a motorman (driver) based at the Barking depot east of London, a convenient journey from his home in New Cross. In 1975 he was not pleased to be transferred to the less convenient Drayton Park depot on the Northern City Line into Moorgate via Highbury and Old Street but by 28th February he had been told that he was to be transferred back to Barking. As he set off to work that morning, therefore, he had every reason to be pleased with his immediate prospects. He was planning a holiday in America and had made enquiries about buying a second-hand Ford Zephyr car for his daughter. A creature of habit he shaved, as always, in the kitchen and packed his tea, coffee and lunch before setting off for the early shift. By 8.39am, as his train left Drayton Park, he had already completed several trips on the short journey from Drayton Park to Moorgate. Seven minutes later his train entered Moorgate station travelling much faster than it should have been. Two railwaymen on platform 9 recognised Newson, calm and upright, with his hands on the controls as the train proceeded to smash at 40 mph into the concrete tunnel wall beyond the platform end.

For four days police, paramedics and 1,324 men of the London Fire Brigade struggled to remove the dead, dying and injured from the wreckage in the tunnel. Newson's body was the last to be recovered of the 43 dead and 74 injured. Two enquiries followed, one by the Chief Inspecting Officer of Railways, Lieutenant

Colonel McNaughton and the other by Dr David Paul, Coroner to the City of London. There was nothing wrong with the train or track. The guard had not been as alert as he might have been and he came in for some criticism but there was no suggestion that, even if he had been more diligent, he could have averted the accident. The accident had been caused by Newson. There was a small amount of alcohol in Newson's body but this was consistent with the amount that could have been produced by the natural decomposition of his body in a hot tunnel over four days. He was not drunk. There was no reason to suspect suicide though there was some evidence that Newson had overrun a platform earlier the same week with no ill effects. There was some discussion of the possibility that Newson had been struck down by the sudden onset of a rare medical condition, *transient global amnesia* or *akinesis with mutism* but, given the state of Newson's body when it was removed from the train, these could not be identified with any confidence. Having summarised the evidence the Coroner informed the jury that there were four possible verdicts open to them: manslaughter, suicide, accidental death or an open verdict. They returned verdicts of accidental death on all the victims, including Newson. The precise cause of the accident remains a mystery.

# Accidents and Tragedies

## THE KINGS CROSS FIRE

In 1981 a fire caused by burning rubbish was responsible for the death of one person and a subsequent enquiry established that, over a thirty-two year period, forty-six fires had occurred on wooden escalators. Of these, thirty-two were caused by smokers discarding matches and cigarettes. London Transport therefore introduced a ban on smoking on Underground platforms and this ban, which was intended to be experimental and possibly temporary, may have led to the disastrous fire at Kings Cross underground station on 18th November 1987. Because of the ban, passengers tended to light cigarettes as they ascended the wooden escalators and it was a discarded match on a Piccadilly Line escalator which caused the fire which killed thirty-one people and injured a further sixty. The match fell through a gap in the escalator and ignited the debris beneath which was coated in grease and, in the words of the report, represented 'a seed bed for a fire'. The fire spread quickly, its thick fumes blocking the exit and killing many victims. The dead included Firefighter Colin Townsley who stopped to assist a distressed passenger and succumbed to smoke inhalation.

Some disturbing facts emerged from the enquiry which followed The Kings Cross fire of 1987 including:

- The area beneath the escalator had not been cleaned since the equipment was installed in the 1940s.

- Most other wooden escalators had similar debris (paper, human and rat hair and other inflammable substances) beneath them.

- Many similar fires had occurred before and had fortunately burned themselves out without any casualties resulting.

- The Underground management's attitude to the problem was fatalistic: this sort of minor fire was bound to happen and there wasn't much one could do about it as long as no-one was hurt.

Thirty-one deaths amounted to sufficient hurt for two major consequences to follow. First, smoking was banned throughout the network. Second, the government was pressured to provide money to replace wooden escalators, though this was partly at the expense of investment in new rolling stock.

# Underground Curiosities

## GHOST STATIONS, MYTHS & LEGENDS

Several underground stations have closed, while one never opened. This was North End station between Hampstead and Golders Green on the Northern Line. Yerkes' Hampstead Tube built a station there in the belief that it would stimulate residential development and profitable long-distance commuters but Henrietta Barnett succeeded in purchasing land adjacent to the station and incorporating it into Hampstead Heath, thereby preventing any buildings being erected. This ensured that the station was never opened though the platforms and other structures underground were completed. It is used for storing engineers' materials. The station is referred to by Underground staff as 'The Bull and Bush' after the pub, famous in song, which stands nearby.

North End station enjoyed a brief moment of fame during World War II when, according to Winston Churchill's account, 'a citadel for the War Cabinet had been prepared near Hampstead with offices and bedrooms and wired and fortified telecommunications. This was called *Paddock*. According to Churchill the facility was used once, on 29th September 1940 when, according to a man who was on Home Guard sentry duty near the unused station, 'Mr Churchill popped out of the ground at my feet'. Above the

**HENRIETTA BARNETT**
(1851–1936) came from a wealthy family but devoted her life to improving the housing and education of the poor, particularly in the East End of London. She was active in founding the Whitechapel Art Gallery and the university settlement at Toynbee Hall. She also founded the Hampstead Garden Suburb, which was designed to provide affordable housing for all. She was awarded the CBE for her work in 1917.

platforms, on the surface, is a small white building which is ostensibly an electricity sub-station but is in fact an emergency exit from the platforms beneath. It was presumably from this that Churchill emerged to startle the Home Guard.

Another station used occasionally by the War Cabinet, though more often by the Railway Executive, was Down Street on the Piccadilly Line between Hyde Park Corner and Green Park. It was never much used and closed in 1932. Its facilities were concealed by a brick wall lest they be seen by German spies in passing trains. London's Transport Museum occasionally takes parties of visitors to this ghostly relic. Six other disused Underground stations were adapted for wartime use including Brompton Road station (between Knightsbridge and South Kensington) which became the headquarters of London's anti-aircraft batteries.

> The oldest disused station on the network is the one at King William Street, just north of London Bridge, which was the original terminus of the City and South London Railway. It was closed in 1900 when Bank station opened. This station now lies beneath a large office building and, like many other disused stations and lines, is used as a document and record store.

## EXTRAORDINARY FACT

At the beginning of World War I, an excitable journalist suggested that the King William Street station, and other disused Underground facilities, might conceal armaments, explosives and German spies. A careful search by police, in the first week of August 1914, revealed no lurking Guy Fawkes figures.

### DID YOU KNOW?

On Friday 3rd August 2012 the Underground carried a record (at the time) number of 4.4 million passengers, many of them travelling to the Olympic Games. This was the day before the 'Super Saturday' when Greg Rutherford, Jessica Ennis and Mo Farah won gold medals for Team GB.
The record now stands at over 5 million journeys on a single day, set in December 2018.

# Underground Curiosities

The prize for the most persistent myth must be awarded to South Kentish Town station, between Camden Town and Kentish Town on the Northern Line. It opened in 1907, was never much used and closed in 1924, following which there arose a story that an absent-minded passenger had alighted at this station when his train was stopped by a signal. He supposedly survived for a week until he caught the attention of a passing train by setting fire to some advertising posters. A more colourful if even less plausible version was given currency by John Betjeman in a radio broadcast of 1951 when the future Poet Laureate claimed that the castaway, a tax inspector, was rescued by a group of workmen who informed him that he was trespassing. As recently as 1997 the story surfaced in a television programme but the mysterious passenger has never been identified. The booking hall, at street level, survives as a graffiti-covered feature of Kentish Town Road, its recent occupants including a massage parlour and a pawnbroker.

AMAZING FACT

The disused Aldwych station, formerly on a branch of the Piccadilly Line, is a popular venue for film sets, having featured in *Battle of Britain*, *The Krays* and *Atonement* amongst others. The last train carrying the general public left Aldwych on the evening of the September 20th 1994.

# FAMOUS NAMES

Some famous names have been associated with stations now lost. British Museum station opened on the Central Line between Tottenham Court Road and Holborn in 1900 but closed in 1933 when Central Line platforms opened at Holborn station. The Museum station is supposedly still visible from passing trains though this passenger has never managed to discern any relics. Another famous name briefly flourished in 1939. In April 1868 the Metropolitan Railway opened St John's Wood Road station between Baker Street and Swiss Cottage, serving Lord's cricket ground nearby. In 1939 the Marylebone Cricket Club (MCC) based at Lord's in St John's Wood, knowing that in 1932 the Underground Group had changed the name of its Gillespie Road station to Arsenal in honour of the football club, suggested that St John's Wood station be renamed Lord's and this duly occurred on 11th June 1939. In November of the same year the Bakerloo opened its own extension to Stanmore with its own St John's Wood station and the Lord's station closed for the duration of the war. It never reopened so Lord's enjoyed this aspect of its celebrity for only five months.

> **EXTRAORDINARY FACT**
>
> In 1909 Gordon Selfridge tried to persuade the Central London Railway to re-name its Bond Street station *Selfridges* after his newly opened department store. He failed.

> **DID YOU KNOW?**
>
> The Metropolitan electrified its services from 1905, though the section beyond Amersham remained steam operated until its transfer to British Rail in September 1961.

# Underground Curiosities

## FOWLER'S GHOST

The problem of designing a locomotive which could run underground without emitting intolerable quantities of steam and smoke in the tunnels engaged the attention of some of the greatest engineers of the day: John Fowler, Robert Stephenson and Isambard Kingdom Brunel. Robert Stephenson, designer with his father George of the famous *Rocket*, was consulted about the feasibility of building a locomotive that could run from Paddington to Farringdon on heat and steam built up in the open before entering the tunnels of the Metropolitan Railway. To reassure the Parliamentary Committee that was considering the proposed railway of the feasibility of this plan, the Metropolitan's chief engineer, John Fowler, produced Brunel himself who reassured the MPs, 'If you are going a very short journey you need not take your dinner with you, or your corn for your horse.' Fowler's design, built by Stephenson and known as 'Fowler's Ghost', stored energy in heated bricks, on the same principle as a storage heater. In 1861 Stephenson delivered the locomotive which, at £4,518, cost about twice as much as a standard engine. It was tested over a seven-mile stretch of the Great Western after which it was dangerously overheated, emitting steam from every orifice, and in danger of exploding. It limped back to its depot and disappeared from history.

> **EXTRAORDINARY FACT**
>
> In 1867, as the Metropolitan Railway extended to Gloucester Road, it became necessary to pass beneath Leinster Gardens in Bayswater. Two houses, numbers 23 and 24, were bought and demolished to enable steam and smoke to be discharged at this point and the facades were later reconstructed, with no house behind them, thus creating endless opportunities for pranks to be inflicted on novice postmen and messenger boys. In 1930 these victims were joined by gullible party-goers who bought £10 tickets for a ball at the address. District and Circle Lines continue to use the cutting.

# THE PNEUMATIC RAILWAY

In 1838 two engineers, Samuel Clegg and Jacob Samuda, patented an 'atmospheric' or pneumatic railway. They built a 2-mile demonstration line at Dun Laoghaire in Ireland which sometimes worked and impressed many who saw it, of whom by far the most important was Isambard Kingdom Brunel, who was constantly seeking new ideas. A cast-iron tube was laid between the rails in which was inserted a piston which was attached to the front of a train. A stationary steam engine at the end of the line pumped out the air ahead of the piston which, with the train attached, was thus drawn into the vacuum and along the rails by atmospheric pressure. Since no smoke or steam was generated by the train itself, the device was eminently suited to trains operating in enclosed spaces. However it depended entirely for its effectiveness upon the creation of an airtight seal around the piston and this proved to be its fatal weakness. Brunel adopted the system for the South Devon Railway in the 1840s, using leather, beeswax and tallow to form the seal but in hot weather the beeswax and tallow melted and in cold weather the leather became stiff and misshapen. A further difficulty attended a similar trial on a railway from London to Epsom when rats developed a taste for the leather seals. The idea was abandoned.

In March 1863 an advertising agent called James Willings paid the new Metropolitan Railway £1,150 for the right to sell books and place advertisements on its stations. Three years later he paid £34,000 for the right to continue the arrangement and he retained the franchise until 1907 when it passed to W.H.Smith. In the meantime he had started to publish *Willing's Press Guide* which remains in use as a authoritative source of information on the press as an advertising medium.

# Underground Curiosities

## THE UNDERGROUND PULLMAN

The early Metropolitan did not really think of itself as an Underground railway: rather as a main line railway which, through painful necessity had to submit to the indignity of travelling underground. For this reason its early rolling stock was indistinguishable from that of a main line railway and this philosophy survived into the twentieth century in the form of the Underground Pullman. The last service departed from Baker Street for Aylesbury at 11.35 pm for theatre-goers. The service survived the absorption of the Metropolitan into the London Passenger Transport Board and continued until the outbreak of war in 1939 when the Pullman cars were converted into moveable homes.

> **EXTRAORDINARY FACT**
>
> On 1st June 1910 the Metropolitan became the first (and so far only) underground railway to introduce a Pullman service, serving breakfast, lunch, afternoon tea and dinner in two Pullman cars called *Mayflower* and *Galatea*.

## ESCALATING FEARS

In October 1911 the first escalator ever on the Underground was installed at Earl's Court station. It was called a 'moving staircase' and was designed so that passengers stepped sideways off the escalator at the top or bottom. *The Times* became lyrical in its description of the novel device:

> *There need be no waiting on the part of the passenger for conveyance to or from the trains. He can step on to the stairlift at once and be gently carried to his train. A boon that the mere*

*man will also appreciate is that he will not be prohibited from smoking, as in the lift, for the stairlift is made entirely of fireproof material.*

The latter claim was, of course, to be disproved in disastrous circumstances at Kings Cross in 1987 but in the meantime the Underground's resourceful Public Relations department could rejoice.

## WHAT'S IN A NAME?

There have, at different times, been three separate Charing Cross stations. The oldest, the main line terminus of the South-Eastern and Chatham Railway, was opened in 1864 on the site of Hungerford market, named after the Somerset based family who owned the land. From 1680 to 1862 the market sold mostly meat, fruit and vegetables but by 1862 it was in decline in the face of markets like Smithfield, Billingsgate and Spitalfields. In that year the site was sold to the South-Eastern Railway from whose station trains departed across Hungerford Railway Bridge to destinations in Kent. In 1870 the District Railway opened a second Charing Cross station on the Victoria Embankment; and in 1907 the Charing Cross, Euston and Hampstead Railway (CCEHR) opened its own Charing Cross terminus north of the District Line station. In 1914 the CCEHR built an extension south to cover the short distance between its Charing Cross and that of the District and, to avoid confusing passengers, changed the name of its station to Strand.

## AMAZING FACT

Passengers were nervous of the first escalator and it is not clear whether they were reassured or further alarmed by the spectacle that greeted many of them on the first day that it came into use. This was the sight of a one-legged man called Bumper Harris riding up and down the new contraption. The missing leg had been lost in an accident many years earlier and the myth that the management had paid him to use the escalator ran for many years until disavowed by one of Bumper Harris's descendants.

# Underground Curiosities

In 1979 the wheel turned again and the redeveloped Strand station became Charing Cross while the former District Line station became Embankment, which more accurately represents its true location.

## GHOSTLY RELICS

Tunnellers on the Victoria Line encountered some fifty-million-year-old fossils now in the Natural History Museum as well as more sinister elements in the form of a plague pit with its accompanying ghost, a seven-foot tall man nicknamed 'The Quare Fellow' by the largely Irish workforce. This wasn't the only ghost reported on the system. In November 1955 a member of the station staff at Covent Garden requested a transfer after seeing a ghostly apparition, six feet tall, pale faced, wearing a light grey suit and white spectacles. Other staff confirmed the sighting. To the *Sunday Dispatch* this sounded like the actor William Terriss, a Victorian actor stabbed to death at the nearby *Adelphi* theatre. A more persistent ghost is the one at Elephant and Castle, where night maintenance staff hear running footsteps. When building the Victoria Line beneath Kings Cross the engineers had to thread it through five existing lines as well as the usual web of sewers, water, gas and electricity pipes. However, since Boadicea,

The construction of the Victoria Line was attended by problems familiar to pioneers such as Marc Brunel, including waterlogged soil on the section between Pimlico and Brixton. However instead of risking the lives and health of the tunnellers by the use of compressed air, as for the Bakerloo Line, the Underground's engineers froze the soil by inserting tubes of liquid nitrogen at temperatures of -200 degrees centigrade.

who is reputedly buried beneath platform ten of the main line station, did not appear to protest, we must assume that her grave was undisturbed by the work.

## THE WIGHT STUFF

In 1965 the Chief Mechanical and Electrical Engineer of the Southern Region of British Rail informed the Southern's General Manager, David McKenna, that the locomotives and rolling stock of the Isle of Wight Railway were nearing the end of their lives. One of the first class carriages, with its ivory-inlaid table, had been used by Queen Victoria. It was not possible to employ locomotives or rolling stock from the mainland because the tunnels on the island were too low to accommodate them. Nor was it acceptable to close the line even though the 55 miles that the island had originally enjoyed had fallen to an 8-mile stretch between Ryde Pier Head and Shanklin. The line was heavily used for a few hours each day during school terms by schoolchildren; and for holidaymakers at summer weekends arriving from the mainland for their holidays in the resorts of Sandown and Shanklin. British Rail therefore bought from London Underground forty-three units of 1938 stock which were converted to run on the island and the new service began in March 1967. In 1984 a further

thirty-four units of 1938 stock were purchased. Visitors arriving at Ryde Pier Head are therefore faced with the bizarre sight of what are clearly recognisable as Underground trains though they have been repainted with colourful seaside scenes. These survivors of the pre-nationalisation era of Lord Ashfield and Frank Pick were clearly built to last.

## THE BRILL TRAMWAY

In December 1935 readers of the correspondence columns of *The Times* would have been intrigued by letters lamenting the demise of a forgotten corner of Sir Edward Watkin's Metropolitan ambitions. In 1891 Watkin had acquired the Aylesbury and Buckingham Railway as part of his plan to create a network of railways, chaired by him, which would enable passengers to travel from Manchester to Paris via London. With this acquisition came the Brill Tramway which ran from the hub of the Watkin empire at Quainton, Bucks to the tiny hilltop village of Brill in the Vale of Aylesbury, a community so remote that it was later chosen by the Great Train Robbers as a hideout at nearby Leatherslade farm. The Brill Tramway had originally been planned by the Duke of Buckingham to run from Aylesbury, via Quainton to a terminus at Magdalen Bridge, Oxford, but even in the heady days of Victorian optimism about railways it never went beyond Brill. The carriages had been drawn by a

AMAZING FACT

The Brill Tramway was mostly used to collect milk churns from farms in the area, shunting operations being carried out by a horse.

mixture of traction engines, a chain-driven miniature steam engine and finally by one of Daniel Gooch's 'condensing' engines. Traces of the line can still be seen on old maps and the ruined remains of stations and other installations are incongruously situated in the middle of fields, surrounded by puzzled sheep.

> A correspondent to *The Times* recalled that, during the frequent derailments, the few passengers would disembark and push the carriages back on to the rails with the assistance of farm labourers.

## THE POST OFFICE RAILWAY

In 1855 Rowland Hill (1795-1879) who had introduced the Penny Post and the accompanying *Penny Black* stamp fifteen years earlier, proposed the construction of a pneumatic tube between the headquarters of the Post Office at St Martin's le Grand and a post office in nearby Holborn. Accordingly, in 1859 the *Pneumatic Despatch Company* was established, its board of directors including the chairman of the London and North Western Railway, based at Euston, and W.H.Smith who was seeking an efficient method of distributing newspapers and magazines to his shops. An oval tube was constructed at Battersea, 452 yards long and about 3 feet in diameter. At one end air was blown into the tube while at the other it was sucked out, causing a partial vacuum which enabled wagons, with a moderately efficient airtight seal, to be drawn along the tube on rails. The experiment was sufficiently encouraging to lead to the construction of a similar tube, 2 feet in diameter, between Euston station and a post office in Eversholt street about 400 yards away. The tube opened in February, 1863, a month after the Metropolitan

# Underground Curiosities

Railway and was used by 30 mail trains each day. *The Times* was ecstatic, optimistically proclaiming that:

> *The days ought to be fast approaching when the ponderous goods vans which now ply between station and station shall disappear for ever from the streets of London.*

The new device became an attraction for distinguished visitors one of whom, Prince Jerome Napoleon, nephew of the former emperor, took a ride along it. However, familiar problems soon arose with maintaining an airtight seal and this, along with road improvements associated with Sir Joseph Bazalgette making it more attractive to use the roads, meant that in 1882 it ceased to be used for mail and was eventually adopted by the Post Office as a conduit for telephone lines.

In 1913 Asquith's cabinet authorized the construction of a 2 foot gauge railway to carry mail from Paddington to Whitechapel via the main sorting office at Mount Pleasant. It eventually cost £1.7 million, twice the original estimate, and opened in 1927, the partly-completed tunnels being used during World War I to house the Elgin Marbles and other artistic treasures. The trains were driverless, controlled like a model railway from the stations en route and few people knew of its existence until 1954 when Brian Johnston took a break from cricket commentary to travel through it carrying a parcel from the BBC headquarters in Portland Place to Bristol. It closed in May 2003 as an economy measure,

Post Office management having concluded that road transport was cheaper.

# ON FOOT TO ALBERTOPOLIS

One of the strangest features of the Underground is the 500 yard long pedestrian subway which runs beneath Exhibition Road from South Kensington Underground station to the Science Museum, serving also the Natural History Museum and the Victoria and Albert Museum en route. The land for the museums and the Albert Hall was originally acquired with the profits from the very successful Great Exhibition of 1851 and, in deference to the Prince Consort who had conceived the idea of the Exhibition, the area was for some time known as Albertopolis. As the museums district took shape, the two railways which served South Kensington station, the Metropolitan and the District, realised that the new attractions were a potential source of passengers. However South Kensington station was about half a mile from the Albert Hall, access to it being via the notoriously

## THE ALBERT HALL SUBWAY

The subway's engineer was John Wolfe-Barry (1836-1918) who is better remembered as the engineer of Tower Bridge. The tunnel was lit by the construction of clerestories opening into Exhibition Road and by electricity, one of the first uses of electric lighting in London. In 1940 the subway was converted into an air raid shelter accommodating 900 people and, when the worst of the air raids had ended, in 1942, about two thirds of the space was taken over by the RAF as a signals school. After the war the subway resumed its role as a traffic-free and weatherproof route for pedestrians and in 2006 it was listed by English heritage as a Grade II structure.

# Underground Curiosities

crowded Exhibition Road with what one contemporary described as its population of 'cab-callers, hawkers and other objectionable characters'. Accordingly the Metropolitan Railway applied to Parliament for powers to build the *Albert Hall Subway*, half a mile long, to accommodate trains or trams which would convey people from South Kensington to the Hall itself. This project proved to be unviable but the rival District Railway secured authority to build the present pedestrian tunnel which takes visitors as far as the entrance to the Science Museum. The subway was built rapidly, between January and May 1885, just in time to serve the *Inventions Exhibition* which opened in that month in the Society's gardens. Railway passengers could use the subway free of charge while other pedestrians had to pay a penny for a single trip, a charge justified by the construction cost of over £42,000. The charge was abolished in 1908.

## OUT-OF-HOURS DRINKING AND RIVERS ACROSS RAILS

For many years certain underground stations were almost unique in offering facilities for out of hours drinking. In 1864, one year after the Metropolitan Railway opened, Felix Spiers and Christopher Pond, who had made a fortune providing food and drink for prospectors during the Ballarat gold rush in Australia, signed an agreement to run refreshment rooms on Metropolitan stations, paying 10 per cent of takings or a minimum of £4,000 a year. Similar arrangements were made for other lines and at one time there were over thirty licensed buffets, many of them remaining open even when pubs were closed as the part of restrictions on licensing hours introduced during World War I.

Liverpool Street had a licensed bar on the eastbound Metropolitan Line platform known as 'Pat-Mac's Drinking Den' which survived until 1978 and is now a café. Another, on the Westbound platform at Sloane Square survived until 1985 and is now a convenience store. Both are celebrated in 'A Word Child' by Iris Murdoch. The buffet at Sloane square also appears in Evelyn Waugh's *Vile Bodies* as a favoured meeting place for 'the latest modern artistic fraternity,' according to the extremely unreliable gossip columnist 'Mr Chatterbox'.

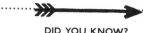

**DID YOU KNOW?**

Sloane Square station has a feature which is unique in the Underground: a river flowing above the tracks. Above the trains is a large metal cylinder running across the lines. This is the river Westbourne which rises on Hampstead Heath, surfaces in Hyde Park as the Serpentine, crosses Sloane Square station in this culvert and enters the Thames at Chelsea.

## A STORY TOO GOOD TO BE TRUE

On the evening of 13th May 1924 Mrs Daisy Hammond gave birth to a baby girl while travelling on a Bakerloo Line train. The event was reported in the *Evening Standard* which enquired of Albert Stanley, who since 1920 had been Baron Ashfield, whether he would become the child's godfather. With some apprehension he agreed, adding 'Of course it would not do to encourage this sort of thing as I am a busy man'. The press was carried away by the story, proposing that the child be named *Louise Baker* and later reporting that she had been christened **T**helma **U**rsula **B**eatrice **E**leanor. Sadly, the story was too good to last and in July 2000 the object of the story assured a television audience that she had in fact been christened Mary Ashfield Eleanor and that she didn't like travelling on the tube. An understandable aversion given the circumstances of her birth.

# Underground Curiosities

## STRANGE SMELLS

Reference has been made elsewhere to the ordeals of passengers caused by emissions of smoke and steam in the tunnels of the Metropolitan and District Railways but the problems did not altogether disappear with electric trains. Unpleasant odours were a source of complaint on the Central London Railway within a few weeks of its opening but more than a year passed before the board felt impelled to do something. An MP suggested that 'delicate people, ladies and others' were reluctant to travel on the line because of the air. A huge fan was installed at the Wood Lane (White City) end of the line but the problem was not solved until clean, ozonised air was pumped into the tunnels in 1911.

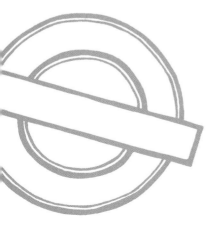

The Reverend Professor George Henson of the Royal Horticultural Society suggested that the carbonic acid which he believed to be the cause of the smell in the Underground could be removed by placing 'evergreen shrubs with plenty of leaf surface such as hollies, rhododendrons etc. on the station platforms' though how they would have flourished in the sunless depths of the Underground was not clear.

# PLEASE KEEP MOVING

At Charing Cross (now Embankment) which was then the busiest station on the system, stentorphones (megaphones) were used through which passengers on the escalators were instructed:

> *Please keep moving. If you MUST stand, then stand on the RIGHT. Some are in a hurry. Don't impede them.*

Presumably the long-suffering passengers were more tolerant of this treatment than the company deserved since a second stentorphone was installed at Oxford Circus shortly afterwards. Lord Ashfield had mixed feelings about this overcrowding. Although he agreed with Sir Edgar Speyer that 'straphangers meant dividends' he took a censorious view of the reason for the overcrowding. In 1924 he wrote, 'One contributory cause has been the emancipation of women, who are tending to travel as freely as men…Another contributory cause is a greater addiction to pleasure.' That would never do!

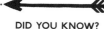

**DID YOU KNOW?**

The famous statue of Eros was moved to the Victoria Embankment while the ticket hall at Piccadilly Circus station was being built.

## EXTRAORDINARY FACT

By 1919, overcrowding on the Underground had led the management to introduce 'hustlers' at Victoria station on the District and Circle Line where the large numbers of commuters arriving from the mainline station struggled to board Underground trains to take them to their final destinations. A 'hustler' stood menacingly on each platform with a stopwatch which he started as soon as the train stopped. After thirty seconds, the hustler sounded a siren which was the signal for the train doors to close even if long-suffering passengers were still struggling to embark.

# Underground Curiosities

## HEALTH AND SAFETY

Victorian and Edwardian attitudes towards health and safety are alarmingly illustrated by an incident which occurred during the early days of the construction of the Bakerloo Line before the demise of Whitaker Wright. While tunnelling through the waterlogged soil beneath the Thames between Charing Cross and Waterloo the shafts leading to the tunnels were sealed with airlocks and compressed air was pumped into the airtight chamber to hold at bay the water in the surrounding soil. Tunnelling then continued in this atmosphere of compressed air. In 1908 the consequences were described at the Institution of Civil Engineers:

> *A great deal of illness resulted among the men but* there were not many fatal cases *(author's emphasis!). The air escaping through the gravelly bed of the river boiled three feet above the surface. It came in the path of a race from Charing Cross to Putney and upset one of the competitors' boats.*

The speaker commented on the compensation that had been paid to the boat owner but illness and mortality amongst the tunnellers seem to have been accepted as some of life's little hazards.

### AMAZING FACT

Underground tunnels used to be cleaned by an army of formidable people, mostly ladies, known as 'fluffers' who descended into the tunnels after the passage of the last train at night, armed with face masks, brooms and dust pans.

## THE BIG YELLOW DUSTER

The greatest threat to the wildlife of the Underground is the *Big Yellow Duster* which is used to remove the debris left behind by the four million passengers who use the network each day. Most of this consists of human tissue, especially hair and skin cells, which we discard unknowingly, to which is added the litter of paper, plastic, food and other substances which are inseparable from twenty-first century life. Until the 1970s this potential fire hazard was removed by human hand. The job is now done by the Tunnel Cleaning Train, built at Acton Works, painted bright yellow and known as The Big Yellow Duster. One set of nozzles blows debris into the air and another sucks it from the atmosphere into containers as the unit makes its way, at 6 mph, around the network. In 1982 it was joined by another device for clearing tracks of leaves, on the stretch between Rickmansworth and Amersham on the Metropolitan Line which, because of the high incidence of lineside trees in this part of 'Beechy Bucks.' is particularly vulnerable to leaf fall.

### DID YOU KNOW?

Tunnellers working underneath the Thames suffered from 'the bends', a painful and sometimes fatal condition. to which submariners are vulnerable when escaping from the deep.

# Index

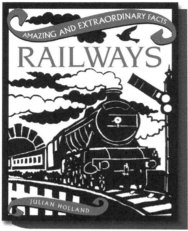

Amazing and Extraordinary
Facts: Railways
Julian Holland
ISBN: 978-1-910821-00-8

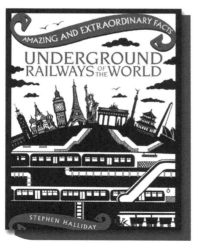

Amazing and Extraordinary
Facts: Underground Railways
of the World
Stephen Halliday
ISBN: 978-1-910821-40-4

Amazing and Extraordinary
Facts: Titanic
Stuart Robertson
ISBN: 978-1-910821-19-0

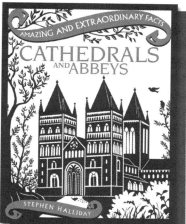

Amazing and Extraordinary
Facts: Cathedrals and Abbeys
Stephen Halliday
ISBN: 978-1-910821-04-6

For more great books visit our website at **www.rydonpublishing.co.uk**

# The Author

Stephen Halliday is a historian specialising in British, industrial and military history. He is an authority on the history of London with a special interest in its great engineering works, and he is the author of several books about London and the Underground including a number of titles from Rydon Publishing's bestselling *Amazing and Extraordinary Facts* series. He also contributes articles and reviews to magazines such as *Literary Review, Times Higher Education, BBC History* and *History Today*.

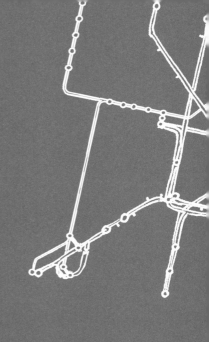